Raymond Keene is a chess grandmaster and chess correspondent of the prestigious London publications *The Times*, *The Sunday Times* and *The Spectator*. He is the author of over 160 books on subjects such as chess, puzzles, genius and brainpower. He has organised three World Chess Championships as well as numerous Memory Championships and Mind Sports events.

Byron Jacobs is a chess international master and a journalist, author and publisher specialising in mind games. He has written extensively on chess, poker, puzzles and Mind Sports in general.

T0168171

# puzzle books from D&B publishing

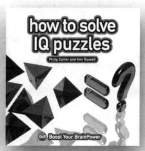

# THE ❦ TIMES

THE SQUARE BOOK OF IQ PUZZLES

## RAY KEENE & BYRON JACOBS

D&B PUBLISHING

www.dandbpublishing.com

First published in 2010 by D & B Publishing

Puzzles included in this book have previously been published in *The Times: Two Brains* (D&B Publishing 2003).

**British Library Cataloguing-in-Publication Data**
A catalogue record for this book is available from the British Library.

ISBN 978 1 904468 53 0

All sales enquiries should be directed to:
D & B Publishing, e-mail: info@dandbpublishing.com,
Website: www.dandbpublishing.com

*The Times* is a registered trademark of Times Newspapers Limited,
a subsidiary of News International Plc.

Cover design by Horatio Monteverde.
Printed and bound in the US by Versa Press.

# CONTENTS

# INTRODUCTION

Raymond Keene's column on IQ and puzzles is published each week and features numerous brain teasers, frequently submitted by readers. Over the past few years, many fascinating puzzles have been published in the column and a substantial forum has developed with people writing in to claim that answers given are controversial or to point out possible alternative solutions. The email address associated with the column regularly receives around substantial emails per week as well as numerous communications by post.

Of all the puzzles that have been published over the years, the one which has been responsible for the largest reader reaction is the following:

> You are in a quiz show with a chance to win a million dollars by selecting the correct box from three. The host – and this is *very* important – knows which box contains the million. You make your choice and then the host opens one of the other boxes to reveal it as empty. He then offers you the chance to change your mind and select the remaining box. Should you do this?

You may wish to consider the problem yourself before looking up the solution. This problem can be found as number 97 in Test Two and the solution is given on page 221.

This question generated an extraordinary response with many readers – including professional mathematicians – claiming that the answer given was nonsense. However, this is not the first time that this question has elicited such a response. In his book *Taking Chances* (Oxford University Press), John Haigh recounts how Marilyn vos Savant, said to have the highest IQ in the world, gave a correct explanation of this puzzle to the readers of her 'Ask Marilyn' column in *Parade* Magazine. The reaction was more or less the same. As Haigh writes: 'Her postbag bulged with excited letters, some from professors in university statistics departments, asserting that she was wrong.'

This puzzle also bamboozled the Hungarian Paul Erdos, who was one of the most brilliant and successful mathematicians of the 20th century. In his biography of Erdos, *The Man Who Loved only Numbers* (4th Estate), Paul Hoffman relates how Erdos was posed the problem by his colleague Andrew Vazsonyi and got the answer wrong. When he was told the correct answer and given the explanation, he simply refused to believe it. He walked away and eventually began to get quite agitated about it. Hoffman wrote: 'Vazsonyi had seen this reaction before, in his students, but he hardly expected it from the most prolific mathematician of the 20th century.'

This goes to show the incredible fascination that brainteasers and puzzles in logic can generate. We hope you enjoy this collection of the best of the problems published in *The Times*.

Raymond Keene and Byron Jacobs
May 2010.

# TEST ONE

Land is to sea as ......... is to strait?

Insert the missing number:

| 2 | 4 | 8 | 4 |
|---|---|---|---|
| 6 | 5 | 3 | 10 |
| 4 | 3 | ? | 8 |

Insert the missing number:

| 16 | | 11 |
|----|---|----|
| | 9 | |
| 25 | | 14 |
| | 13 | |
| 16 | | 5 |
| | ? | |

What is the missing number?

6, 7, 9, 8, ?, 8, 6

Tri is to sex as quad is to .........?

What is the next number in this sequence?

4, 19, 49, 109, ???

What is the next number in this sequence?

4, 5, 8, 17, 44, ???

What is the next number in this sequence?

4, 4, 5, 13, 40, ???

Who comes next?

Harold, James, Michael, Neil, John, ???

Which of the following words are bogus?

Atoks, Cruve, Emf, Nauplii, Plongs, Woktu

Ten letters have been randomly allocated different values from 0 to 9. The sum of the letter values in GAMMA is 30, in ETA is 11, THETA 23, IOTA 20, PI 12 and PHI 20. What are the values of ALPHA and OMEGA?

In the following sum each of the digits from 0 to 9 is used. Given that S + V = E, can you make the sum work?

```
  A
CAT
HAS
NINE
-----
LIVES
```

When you place a pan of water on the cooker, what method transfers the heat to the water?

Radiation, Conduction, Thermal, Convection, Molecular

Match the following names and numbers:

Polyphemus, Sleipnir, Briareos, Shelob, The Kraken

100, 8, 1, 10, 8

What is the next number in this sequence?

3, 4, 6, 12, 36, ?

The two statements below can be read as two professions. What are they?

a) GO NURSE         b) MOON STARER

What numbers can replace these letters?

ABCDEF × 3 = BCDEFA

Which letter is next in this series?

O T T F F S S

If DG = 53 and FT = 406, what does TC equal?

Name two five-letter words which use four different vowels plus the letter 'd'.

What numbers can replace these letters? (No 0 or 3)

```
  ABC
+ BDG
----
  EFGB
```

What animal's name can be formed by using all of these letters?

a, e, m, m, o, r, s, t

If FRIDAY = 63 and SUNDAY = 84, what day = 100?

Can you think of people's names which answer these clues?

a) Highly coloured variety of quartz?
b) Evergreen: emblem of love?
c) Plant of the mint family?
d) French gold coin?

Why is this a Christmas greeting?
ABCDEFGHIJKMNOPQRSTUVWXYZ

What substance is denoted here?

HIJKLMNO

A census taker comes to a house and asks how many people live there. He is told there are three. Then he asks what their ages are and is told that the product of the three ages is 200 and the sum of the three ages is the number of the house. The census taker then thinks a while and says: 'I cannot figure out the ages from this information. I must ask another question: is there someone in the house over 21?' The answer is yes and now the census taker knows the three ages. What are they?

Gaggle is to Geese as Pod is to .........?

If
ENGLAND = 4623165
LEG = 453
DANGLE = 738456

what does AND equal?

Pride is to Lions as ......... is to Crows?

What are the two square roots of 28,355,625?

Party (.........) Sphere

What missing word has the same meaning as the two outer words?

Which Shakespearean character called whom 'juggling fiends'?

A man weighing 140 pounds wishes to cross a bridge that will take a maximum weight of 150 pounds but will collapse if this is exceeded, even minutely. He has three identical objects, each weighing 5 pounds. Since one object will always be in the air, can he safely cross the bridge by juggling?

Take the following sequence:

8, ?, 4, ?, 1, ?, 6, ?, 2

Insert the missing digits (i.e. 3, 5, 7 and 9 – not 0) in such a way that the resulting sequence is in a simple and logical order.

There are three electric switches on the outside of a sealed room and each works a lamp inside. You can turn the switches on or off as you like but you are allowed to look inside or go inside the room only once. How can you decide which switch works which lamp?

If FDB + CEG = III, what is missing from the following sum?

EHA + ??? = III

(Note: the answer to both sums consists of three capital 'I's, not 1s)

Which other letter of the alphabet will belong with the following group?

B, C, D, E, G, P, T

If R + Y = O and B + R = P, what does Y + B = ?

What number is missing from this sequence?

4, 7, ?, 18, 29, 47

Complete the following sentence with two different seven-letter words. The words used must be anagrams, i.e. the same seven letters must be used for both words.

He has been her ? on ? occasions.

If OXFORD = 60, YORK = 275 and INVERNESS = 171, what does MANCHESTER = ?

Which of these words does not belong with the others?

CIVIC, FEWER, RADAR, LEVEL and REFER

In a restaurant a man orders a meal and a drink. The bill comes to £11. If the meal costs £10 more than the drink, how much does the drink cost?

'Time's running past we murmur'

is an anagram of four words connected to each other and the sentence. What are the words?

If CHARLES is 50, SYLVESTER is 45 and KEVIN is 4, how old is LOUISE?

What letter should come next in this series?

J, F, M, A, M, ?

If Sam gives Chloe three sweets they will both have the same number of sweets. If Chloe gives Sam three sweets Sam will have four times as many sweets as Chloe. How many sweets each do Chloe and Sam have?

At the Annual General Meeting of the Dead Poets Society a steward mixed up the letters of some of the delegates' names. Can you help out by giving the correct names?

TOILETS, NERDDY, TOMNIL, EASESHEPARK

One of the poets from Question 49 wrote the following. Can you identify this quotation?

'They say there's but five upon this isle: we are three of them; if the other two be brain'd like us the state totters.'

Place the following in chronological order from most recent to most distant.

CRISTIAS, BROCANISEFOUR, SUJARCIS, TRACESOUCE

Can you identify the following quotation?

'What the hammer? What the chain?
In what furnace was thy brain?'

Can you identify the following quotation?

'... a false creation,
Proceeding from the heat oppressed brain'

Find the missing number:

35    37    13    5    3
  36    25    9    ??

If earth = 1, match the following names and numbers.

Neptune, Uranus, Saturn, Jupiter

18, 8, 16, 15

| Test One | MORE PLANETS | Question 56 |
|---|---|---|

If earth = 1, match the following names and numbers.

Pluto, Mars, Venus, Mercury

0.2408, 0.6152, 1.881, 248.5

| Test One | ELEMENTARY | Question 57 |
|---|---|---|

Match these substances with these numbers.

Hydrogen, Helium, Lithium, Carbon, Oxygen

6, 2, 8, 3, 1

| Test One | SATELLITES | Question 58 |
|---|---|---|

Match the following names from the first list with those in the second.

Mars, Jupiter, Saturn, Uranus, Neptune, Pluto
Charon, Titan, Miranda, Io, Triton, Phobos

| Test One | CAST LIST | Question 59 |
|---|---|---|

What word connects the film roles of Professor Higgins, Dr Doolittle, Han Solo and Indiana Jones?

| Test One | BEAR | Question 60 |
|---|---|---|

Can you identify the following quotation and who said it?

'I am a Bear of Very Little Brain, and long words Bother me.'

What is the approximate weight of the average human brain?

Who said the following and where?

'In my youth,' Father William replied to his son,
'I feared it might injure the brain;
But now that I'm perfectly sure I have none,
Why, I do it again and again.'

What is the potential number of connections for one brain cell?

$10^5, 10^{15}, 10^{28}, 10^{47}$

What do we call a brain cell:

synapse, axon, dendrite or neuron?

'A man should his keep his little brain attic stocked with all the furniture that he is likely to use, and the rest he can put away in the lumber-room of his library.' What is the source?

What is the next number in this sequence?

VII, V, VIII, VI, ??

---

At the annual conference of the Brain Users Association, the signs for the lectures on cinematography, geology, classical Greek statues and osteology became jumbled. Can you help?

BRAIN FOFILE, MAC BRAIN, ELMSLEG BRAIN, MUMU BRAIN

---

What is the product of the shortest numbers of moves for a chess knight to travel from the square b1 to reach h8 and the shortest number of moves for a knight to reach b6 from g1?

---

Can you match these substances with these numbers?

Hydrogen, Carbon, Nitrogen, Oxygen, Helium
14, 16, 12, 4, 1

---

Who said and where?

'The brain of this foolish-compounded clay, man, is not able to invent anything that tends to laughter, more than I invent, or is invented on me: I am not only witty in myself, but the cause that wit is in other men.'

Who wrote and where?

'The petrifactions of a plodding brain.'

If (Venus + Earth) × Neptune = 40, how much is (Jupiter − Mercury) × Pluto?

Who said?

'Memory – the warder of the brain.'

If (Henry × Edward) − William = 60, how much is (Richard + Stephen) × Charles?

Those brain users are still at it. At the Braintree Local Association meeting they once again muddled up the signs for their lecture topics. Can you help?

African Studies, Middle Eastern Studies, Modern Cartoon Techniques, Latin American Studies

OI BRAIN, AH BRAIN, ADL BRAIN, USE BRAIN SOE

Number A is of indeterminate length but ends in 4. Number B has the same number of digits as A, starts with 4 and is 4 times the size of A. Using this information alone, can you work out both numbers?

Can you match the following?

Wellington, Cardigan, Caesar, Kutuzov, Marlborough

Borodino, Blenheim, Waterloo, Balaklava, Alesia

In a pitch battle at dead of night a strategically important bridge will be blown up in 40 minutes. Four soldiers must cross to the other side in safety but only two can travel at any given moment and there is only one lamp between them. Soldier A takes one minute to cross, soldier B five minutes, soldier C fifteen minutes and soldier D twenty. What is the optimum sequence for crossing the bridge?

Can you complete the following sentences?

Marx is to Communism as Darwin is to ..........?
Einstein is to relativity as Cuvier is to ..........?
Nelson is to Victory as Columbus is to ..........?
Kirk is to Enterprise as Jason is to ..........?

| Test One | ROYAL MEANS | Question 80 |
| --- | --- | --- |

If the average of Victoria, Elizabeth I and Mary I is 1649, what is the average of John, George I and William I?

| Test One | NAME LINKS | Question 81 |
| --- | --- | --- |

Which name links the following?

Groan, Oates, Andronicus, Flavius Sabinus Vespasianus?

| Test One | QUEENS | Question 82 |
| --- | --- | --- |

How many queens can be placed on an open chessboard of 64 squares without any threatening any other, and what are the optimal squares?

| Test One | PERRY | Question 83 |
| --- | --- | --- |

Distinguish between the following:

Frederick John Perry, Matthew Perry, Perry Mason, Perry White, The Peer and the Peri.

| Test One | MIDDLE AGES | Question 84 |
| --- | --- | --- |

The product of the ages of three ex-teenagers is 17,710. Find their ages.

| Test One | DIETS | Question 85 |
| --- | --- | --- |

Dietary habits.

Lion is to wildebeest as giraffe is to .........?

Look at the following sequence of numbers:

2, 3, ?, 7, 11, 13, ?, 19

Fill in the gaps, and then calculate the product of the entire sequence. For genius credit do not use a calculator or pen and paper.

Link the names in the first list with those in the second list:

Howard, Nelson, Don John, Themistocles, Howe
Aboukir, Salamis, The Armada, Ushant, Lepanto

During a total electricity blackout you are picking handkerchiefs and wish to make sure that you have at least two of one colour. The choices are yellow, pink, white, brown and blue. How many handkerchiefs do you need to pick, sight unseen?

What is the word inside this circle?

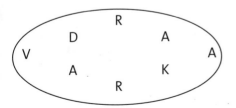

Athlete 4 always beats Athlete 1, while Athlete 2 beats 3, but loses to Athlete 1. Who finishes last?

What are the next two numbers in this sequence?

6, 12, 24, 30, 60, 66, 132, ??, ??

Hannibal is to Zama as Napoleon is to .........?

What are the next two numbers in this sequence?

97, 106, 99, 108, 101, 110, 103, ??, ??

In what respect should an illustration of the Biblical Adam differ anatomically from any other man?

$(X - 4) / 8 = Y$
$(X + 6) / 10 = Y$
What is X?

| Test One | WINDOW SHOPPING | Question 96 |

Window shopping in New York you realise that buying item A plus item B costs you $110. Buying item A plus item C costs you $98, while buying item C plus item B costs $114. You only have one British £50 note in your purse but you can change it into dollars at the rate of £1 for $1.6. You want to get the most expensive item. Which is it, how much does each item costs in dollars and how many dollars change do you get?

| Test One | TRUTH AND LIES | Question 97 |

John always lies – Jim always tells the truth. One said: 'The other one says he is John.' Who said this?

| Test One | HUNGRY TORTOISE | Question 98 |

A tortoise is heading for a tasty piece of fresh lettuce at the other end of the garden. The garden is 6 metres long and the tortoise moves at the rate of 1 metre an hour. However, after each hour's advance, the tortoise instantly falls asleep and a naughty boy immediately moves it back half a metre. This at once wakes the tortoise, which proceeds with its advance. How long does it take the tortoise to reach the lettuce?

| Test One | RACE | Question 99 |

In a five way race A came before B but after C. D came before E but after B. What was the final line up?

| Test One | THREE BEARS | Question 100 |

The three bears were having a picnic at a round table in the forest. One ate honey, another berries and the third nuts. Papa bear sat on the right of the berry eater, while mama bear sat to the right of baby bear. Who was eating the berries?

# TEST TWO

A is twice as old as B was when A was as old as B is now. If B is 24, how old is A?

I recently sold four chess sets for a total of £1,600. The Staunton set went for the same price as the Barleycorn and half the price of the Lewis. The Barleycorn sold for the price of the Russian set minus the price of the Lewis. The Lewis was a third the price of the Staunton. The price for the Russian set equalled the total price of the Barleycorn and the Lewis. How much was each set?

The concierge took out half the money hidden in her mattress to buy herself a new vacuum cleaner. Unfortunately, when her wages were late she had to sell it at a loss two months later, receiving back only 75% of the price she had paid. When she stuffed the money back into her mattress she had 300 euros less than she started with. How much did the vacuum cleaner cost?

Three businessmen decided to divide their dinner cost equally, even though they had not consumed items of the same price. The Chairman paid an extra £15. The Vice President paid £21 less than he should, while the CEO, who should have paid £165, had to fork out £6 more. What was the total bill and what should the other two have paid if they had paid exactly for what they had consumed?

A connoisseur of chess sets needed to enlarge the space in his den to increase his collection. He made the display space larger by 50% thus creating room for all the sets he owned plus two more. If each set takes up one square foot of space, how many chess sets does he now own?

At the charity ball, members paid £57.50, while guests paid £95. The sum of £36,250 was raised and 50% more members than guests attended. How many members and how many guests were there?

General A, Colonel B and Major C dined with their wives at a circular table. Husbands and wives alternated but no officer sat next to his wife. If the colonel was two to the right of the major and the colonel's wife two to the right of the major's wife, who sat on the general's right?

Which is the odd one out?

circumference, diameter, radius, hypotenuse, chord

I bought a deluxe Monopoly set but lost a playing piece on the way home and had to go back to the shop for a replacement. Together, the set and the extra piece cost £101. The set cost £100 more than the replacement piece. What did each cost?

Relationships in Norse mythology between Gods, their pets and mortals were very complicated and many legends grew up around them. One legend had it that Odin's eight-legged horse Sleipnir was the product of the union between Odin himself (disguised as a stallion) and fellow God Loki (in the shape of a mare). Another myth has it that Brunnhilde the Valkyrie was Odin's daughter by the earth Goddess, while a third states that Odin was also the father of the mortals Sigmund and Sieglinde, who were brother and sister. The hero Siegfried was the son of this pair and he became betrothed (accidentally) to the Rhine Princess Gutrune. If Siegfried and Gutrune had had a child, what would its relationship have been with:

a) Brunnhilde?          b) Odin's magic horse?

---

**Test Two**                              **WAGNER**                              **Question 11**

To what question might Richard Wagner have reasonably responded '9W!'?

---

**Test Two**                              **BEAM ME UP**                              **Question 12**

On a mission the Starship Enterprise cruised at sub-warp speed between the planet Vulcan and its furthest moon, at 50,000 kilometres per hour. On the return trip it travelled at 75,000 kph. As the trip was slowed down by a meteor shower, it took the Enterprise two hours longer to do the outward journey than the return journey. How far apart are Vulcan and its moon?

---

**Test Two**                              **CHICKEN OR BEEF?**                              **Question 13**

In the sanatorium three inmates, Adolf, Albert and Josef, developed a fixed dining pattern. Each evening the choice was restricted to either chicken or beef. If Adolf has chicken, Albert has beef. Either Adolf or Josef order chicken, but not both. Albert and Josef do not both have beef. Which of the three had chicken one day and beef the next?

---

**Test Two**                              **MONSTER MASH**                              **Question 14**

At the conference on archetypes in literature and myth one lecturer mixed up the notes. Can you correctly associate the following characters with the appropriate monster?

Bilbo Baggins – The Giant Squid
Frodo Baggins – The Lernean Hydra
Hercules – Grendel
Captain Nemo – Smaug the Dragon
Beowulf – Shelob the Spider

After answering the following three questions, add 'a' to 'c' then subtract 'b'.

a)      14     17     20     ??

b)      93     85     77     ??

c)      1      12     12
         3      4      12
         10     20     ??

Can you work out this mix up and assign the right horse to each real or fictional character?

Wellington – Pegasus
Alexander the Great – Incitatus
Caligula – Copenhagen
Odin – Bucephalus
Perseus – Sleipnir

Puzzle 'a' has two possible solutions. Add them together and then multiply the result by the answer from 'b'.

a)   6,   11,   28,   ??
    12,   22,   14,    6

b) I N T 5 L L I ? 5 N C 5

Some inattentive schoolchildren have given imaginative answers to a question asking which object belongs where. Can you sort them out?

Saqqara – Temple of Zeus
Rhodes – The Parthenon
Athens – The Step Pyramid
Moscow – The Lincoln Memorial
Washington – The Kremlin
Olympia – The Colossus

Deduct missing number 'b' from 'a'.

a) 1, 4, 9, 61, 52, 63, 94, ??        b) 9, 11, 21, 23, 33, 35, ??

Whose name is indelibly associated with which battle, either as winner or loser?

Rameses II – Teutoberger Forest
Antony and Cleopatra – Kadesh
Hermann – Actium
Leonidas – The Wilderness
Ulysses S Grant – Thermopylae

All the vowels have been removed from the following saying. Can you reconstruct it?

FLND HSMN YRSN PRTD

On the first day of Christmas my True Love sent to me a Partridge in a Pear Tree. The plan was to continue according to tradition over the 12 days of Christmas with Turtle Doves, French Hens, Calling Birds, Gold Rings, Geese-a-Laying, Swans-a-Swimming, Maids-a-Milking, Ladies Dancing, Lords-a-Leaping, Pipers Piping and Drummers Drumming. However things did not go to plan.

50% of the Partridges were diverted to a top London restaurant; one-third of the French Hens were held up at Calais; 25% of the Gold Rings were snatched by magpies and 35% of the Swans-a-Swimming were being auditioned by Sir David Attenborough. To make matters worse, five Maids-a-Milking eloped with the same number of Drummers Drumming, six of the Ladies Dancing defected from the Royal Ballet to form a new company, and 90% of the Lords-a-Leaping were hereditary peers and lost their seats, so refused to co-operate in protest.

If all had gone according to plan how many gifts would have been received?

Following on from Question 22: how many did I actually get?

The price of winter fuel in Bohemia is subject to market forces, but is – with rare exceptions – inflationary. On Christmas Eve a single log costs 4 groats, while a bundle of 5 logs attracts a 10% discount. There are 100 pfennigs to the groat, the pfennig being the smallest unit of currency and in all calculations any fractions of pfennigs are simply eliminated.

On Christmas Day, the price of both logs and bundles increase by 2%. On Boxing Day the price increases by a further 5% on the new level, while on 27 December the price of both items escalates by a further 10%. Up to and including New Year's Day, the price increases over the previous day's level by a steady 2% each day. However, on 2 January a large shipment of logs arrives from the neighbouring province of Ruritania and the price goes into reverse. Compared with 1 January, prices of individual logs fall by 50% while bundles now attract a 15% discount.

On 2 January, what is the combined cost of three bundles and two logs?

And what would four logs have cost on 30 December?

Starfleet is mobilising for its new year programme of space exploration and Admiral Kirk has ordered a number of important solar system initiatives involving your section. You are told to search for sentient life forms on the following moons in ascending order of their mean distance from the sun: Charon, Titania, Phobos, Triton and Io. Which sequence should you follow?

On your return Admiral Kirk then sends you on a voyage to hunt for life forms on the moons of Venus and Mercury. What conclusion do you draw from this?

If Waterloo multiplied by Trafalgar = 3,276,075 then what are:

a) Marston Moor multiplied by Naseby?        b) Hastings plus Agincourt?

Professor Dodecahedron of the Peloponnese School of Classical Myth has confused his lecture notes on numerology in Greek and Roman legends, and a bright graduate student has had to disentangle his topics from his numbers. Can you do this as well?

The three Labours of Hercules
The twelve Muses
The twenty-four Graces
The nine Books of Homer's Iliad.

A Stakhanovite worker in a 1930s Moscow factory singlehandedly constructed 25 fighter planes in just five weeks, each week constructing 1.5 more aircraft than during the preceding week. What quantity of fighter planes did he put together during his week of activity?

If 6 milkmaids can fill 6 pails of milk in just 6 minutes, how many milkmaids does it take to fill 100 pails in 100 minutes?

On the annual migration of the million-strong herds in the Serengeti plain 80% had body stripes, 650,000 had a black stripe between their horns, 950,000 had striped legs and 750,000 had striped tails. What is the minimum number of animals that were striped in all four areas?

In 2000 the British Chess Federation decided to re-organise its national championship into a 32-player knockout system. How many matches are required between individual players before a winner emerges?

Professor Polonius of the maths department and Dr Mephistopheles of the English Literature facility of Wittenberg University have combined forces to investigate arcane numerology in the English Classics. Can you help them with two gaps in their text?

What is the product of the two missing numbers in the following quotations?

a) 'The ??? natural shocks the flesh is heir to.'
b) 'Was this the face that launched ??? ships and burnt the topless towers of Ilium?'

Wittenberg Museum owns a fine collection of Oriental prints plus one fragment. The decision has been taken by Herr Director Cornelius to catalogue their possessions. Of the total number of prints, 350 are Indian, 160 are Chinese and 45% Japanese. What is the smallest possible total number of full prints in the collection?

Professor Polonius and Dr Mephistopheles are still investigating numerology in the English Classics. Now, though, their team has been strengthened by the addition of Senior Lecturer Lutwidge and Vice Chancellor Alfred. Can you help them with two further gaps?

What numbers do you get when you add the two missing numbers in the following quotations?

a) 'Into the valley of death rode the ???'
b) 'Sometimes I've believed as many as ??? impossible things before breakfast.'

During Sir Galahad's epic quest for the Holy Grail he finally arrived at the Bridge of Doom guarded by a ghastly minion of Morgan le Fay. The Guardian would only let him cross the bridge if the knight could correctly answer the following question: 'Will I let you pass?'

What should Sir Galahad say to get across?

Why does the sequence HIJKLMNO connect the following missing letters?

The Slough of Des????
Sir Percy B????ney
A ??? of troubles

After a severe storm in the prime fishing grounds Captain Haddock's weekly trawling expedition – which normally lasts 15 hours – netted 6/10ths less Dover sole than he was used to catching on one excursion. Presuming the proportion of Dover sole stayed at this level for the rest of the week, how much longer would he need to go fishing during that week to catch his normal quote of Dover sole?

Hubert the Hunter is tracking a bear which is 100 yards due north of him. Hubert moves 100 yards due east from his original position while the bear stays put. Hubert now fires due north from his new position and hits the bear. What colour is the bear?

Hubert sets off at 4pm to walk to his igloo to fetch a sledge to bring back the bear. Walking at 3 miles per hour he reaches his igloo at 7pm. Next day, taking the same route back he leaves his igloo with his sledge, also at 3 miles per hour. Leaving at 4pm and reaching the bear at 7pm does Hubert pass the same point at the same time on the journey to and from the igloo?

The Emperor of Byzantium wanted to build an aqueduct to provide fresh water for the provincial city of Antioch. The source lay 40 miles away and at first the terrain ran downhill. However, the final stretch was uphill. Is it possible for water to flow uphill?

Professor Quaver of the Music Academy got his lecture notes back to front and allowed one unrelated topic to slip in. Can you find the odd one out?

The topics are TRAZOM, HCAB, OSSACIP, RENGAW, RELHAM

Connect the names in group A with the items in group B.

Group A: Shakespeare, Marlowe, Mozart, Milton
Group B: mailbeermat, nilebymce, rapideas stol, lefötuberaz.

Trains run from A to B one a minute, 24 hours a day. Trains run from B to A at the same rate with the journey taking one hour. Travelling from A to B how many trains do you pass?

Seven beakers stand in a row. Number 1 is empty, 2, 3 and 4 are full, while 5, 6 and 7 are empty. What is the quickest way to rearrange the beakers in order to leave them alternately empty and full?

In the 100 step Ziggurat of Ur, priests gathered for the sacrifice to the memory of the hero Gilgamesh. The High Priest stood on the top step, then two acolytes on the second, with lower priests standing three on the third step, four on the fourth step and so on down to the 100th step. However, one priest heading for the bottom step was delayed by an earlier sacrifice at the Temple of Enkidu and did not make it. How many priests were at the ceremony?

On the island of Erewhon the Goblin population, thought to be near extinction, has expanded enormously. We know now two facts about them:

a) There are 400 goblins.

b) No goblin has more than 150 wrinkles on his face.

From this can we deduce that there must be two goblins with the same number of wrinkles?

| Test Two | USED CARS | Question 49 |
| --- | --- | --- |

Beauregarde's Used Cars was offering second-hand vehicles for £1,000 plus 50% of each car's price. How much did the cars cost?

| Test Two | ORIENT EXPRESS | Question 50 |
| --- | --- | --- |

The Orient Express leaves P at the same time as the Romanian Flyer departs from B. The Orient Express travels at 150 kilometres per hour, while the Romanian Flyer speeds along at 175 kilometres per hour. Which train is further from P when they pass?

| Test Two | ONE WORD ANSWER | Question 51 |
| --- | --- | --- |

What do the following words have in common?

DVA, DEUX, ZWEI, DUE, DOS

| Test Two | GREEDY | Question 52 |
| --- | --- | --- |

At Dotheboys Hall Comprehensive School each child is given a bag of sweets containing two gobstoppers, two sherbets, two jelly babies and two caramels. During the morning break seven-tenths eat a gobstopper, 85% a sherbet, four-fifths a caramel and three-quarters a jelly baby. What is the minimum percentage of children who must have eaten all four?

| Test Two | PHILOSOPHY | Question 53 |
| --- | --- | --- |

At his philosophy lectures Professor Synapse gave papers on TANK, TOPAL, RISOLETTA, SNUBER and TTTNNEEIIWSG. Which topic was out of place?

The Transylvanian Flyer is travelling on a 300km stretch of track across central Europe. After 200km the train breaks down and the passengers have to transfer to the Vlad Puffer, a much slower local locomotive. The final 100km takes twice as long as the first 200km. How many times faster was the Transylvanian Flyer than the Vlad Puffer?

Rearrange the following words so that they match:

EINSTEIN – MICROSOFT
DODGSON – GRAVITY
GOETHE – RELATIVITY
NEWTON – LOOKING GLASS
GATES – FAUST

Farmer Giles has to cross a narrow bridge with three sensitive items, but he can only carry one at a time. They are: hungry rabbit, ravenous cat and tasty carrots. Given that the cat will eat the rabbit if given the chance, while the rabbit will devour the carrots if they are left unattended, how does he solve his problem?

Rearrange the following so that they match:

AUSTRALIA – VIENNA
DENMARK – HELSINKI
AUSTRIA – COPENHAGEN
S. KOREA – CANBERRA
FINLAND – SEOUL

| Test Two | CIRCLES | Question 58 |
|---|---|---|

A triangle is composed of ten circles on four levels. Level 1 at the top has one circle, A. Level 2 has two, B and C. Level 3 has three, D, E and F, while level 4 has four, G, H, I and J. What is the minimum number of circles that need to be rearranged so that the apex of the triangle appears at the bottom?

| Test Two | WISE WORDS | Question 59 |
|---|---|---|

Who famously said:
Veni, Vidi, Vici          a) Julius Caesar,      b) Rene Descartes
Arma virumque cano        a) Virgil              b) Nero
Qualis artifex pereo      a) Virgil              b) Nero
Cogito ergo sum           a) Caligula            b) Descartes.

| Test Two | ROMAN MATHS | Question 60 |
|---|---|---|

Divide LXXX by XX, multiply by C and add DC. What is the final figure?

| Test Two | EQUILATERAL | Question 61 |
|---|---|---|

An equilateral triangle has the number 2 at the top, 6 bottom left and 4 bottom right. How do you place the numbers 8, 10, 12, 14, 16 and 18 along the sides so that each side adds up to 34?

| Test Two | CUSTER'S LAST STAND | Question 62 |
|---|---|---|

The night before the Battle of the Little Big Horn Colonel Custer dreamed that he was surrounded in a pure circle by 12 braves and one Indian chief. He had just 13 rounds of ammunition left and could only scare off the attackers by firing around the circle in one direction, either clockwise or anti-clockwise, firing at every 13th assailant. As each Indian was scared off, the size of the circle was reduced by one. The chief had to be saved for the final shot. Where did Custer start so that each bullet was used to maximum effect?

| Test Two | PRONOUNCE THIS | Question 63 |
|---|---|---|

It is obvious how the word 'ghoti' should be pronounced – or is it? Can you justify the pronunciation of 'fish'?

| Test Two | SILENCE | Question 64 |
|---|---|---|

Following on from the previous question, that word 'ghoti' could also be completely silent. Can you justify this?

| Test Two | EXCHANGE RATE | Question 65 |
|---|---|---|

If 12 zloty equal 16 ley, how many zloty are there for 72 ley?

| Test Two | ORDER | Question 66 |
|---|---|---|

Put the following in correct order, starting with the closest to a very large object:

HATER, RAMS, PRETJUI, SNUVE, NATURS, CRUMYER

| Test Two | SUBTRACTION | Question 67 |
|---|---|---|

If you subtract the number of red cards in a normal pack of cards from the number of dark squares on a chessboard, what number is left?

| Test Two | RUSSIANS | Question 68 |
|---|---|---|

General Jackson wants to deploy his divisions to neutralise the presence of the Russians. He orders the 4th para to go to the north of the 3rd para and northwest of the Russians. The Russians are southeast of the 4th para and northeast of the hussars. The tank regiment is northeast of the 3rd para and west of 2nd para. Which troop deployment is north of the Russians?

LUBL is to WOC as TAGS is to WEE, ODE, SWO or CKBU

(Clue: think ungulates!)

If Z + A = 27 and X multiplied by Y = 6 what is I plus T minus M?

Water from a cold tap will take 30 minutes to fill a 600 litre bath. From a hot tap it will take 40 minutes. The full bath takes 50 minutes to empty. If the bath is empty and the plug is out and the hot and cold taps are both turned on, how long will it take to fill the bath?

Cock is to bull as stuff is to ???

If Elizabeth = 3 and George = 21, what do Richard and Charles equal?

Professor Politicus has mixed up leaders and residences. Can you help him out?

Casa Rosada, The Kremlin, The White House, 10 Downing Street
Boris Yeltsin, Bill Clinton, Tony Blair, General Galtieri

Three starships enter space dock. They each need repairs to the hyperdrive and photon torpedo replenishment. There are two teams of star mechanics available, A and B, who operate equally swiftly. It takes 15 hours to repair the hyperdrive and five hours each to arm each starship with photon torpedoes. How quickly can the whole job be done?

Fred and Joe both have £1,000. Fred bets Joe £100 that if Joe gives Fred £200 Fred will give him £300 back. If the transaction proceeds, who will benefit?

A hunter chases a bear for three miles due north and then due south for a further two miles. What is the maximum distance he can be from where he began the hunt?

The Tsar of Russia wanted to fill his lake with 400 gallons of water. However, the imperial water trucks only took 300 or 500 gallons. How could the Tsar engineers measure exactly 400 gallons?

As Napoleon retreated from Moscow he was pursued by General Janvier through deep snow and blinding blizzards. At the first skirmish General Janvier lost 20% of his troops. At the second skirmish he lost 20% of those left. If he lost 7,200 men in total how many did he start with?

---

**DID YOU KNOW?**
89.06 is the percentage of people who report normally writing with their right hand, 10.6% with their left and 0.34% with either hand.

An aeroplane has a speed of 600 mph in still air. It makes a return journey between two points, one leg against a wind of 100 mph and the other with a tailwind, also of 100 mph. What is the average speed over the two journeys?

A rich sheikh has four sons and three daughters, all equestrians. Upon his death they are to have a horse race. The last horse across the finishing line will inherit his fortune. How do they run the race?

Six rhinos can devour six bales of hay in six minutes. The zookeeper gathers 100 bales of hay in his store room and leaves them unguarded for one hour and forty minutes. When he returns all the hay has been consumed. How many rhinos were guilty?

The Cornelius family in Ancient Rome was famous for its longevity. Gaius Cornelius was born in 50BC. Which birthday would he have celebrated in 50AD?

Re-arrange the following famous animal lovers in appropriate pairs:

Hannibal – Cats
T.S. Eliot – Elephants
Hemingway – Apes
Darwin – Big Game

| Test Two | COIN TOSS | Question 85 |
| --- | --- | --- |

Three boys play at tossing a coin. The winner is the first to throw a head. Andrew goes first, Bob second and Colin third. What are their chances?

| Test Two | MATCHSTICK MANIA | Question 86 |
| --- | --- | --- |

V + I = II

How can the above equation be rectified by moving just one matchstick. (There are four possible answers.)

| Test Two | OPPOSITES | Question 87 |
| --- | --- | --- |

Left is to right as top is to bottom, so black is to white as cameo is to .........?

| Test Two | APPOSITES | Question 88 |
| --- | --- | --- |

What specifically do these words have in common?

Pride, Unkindness, Murder

| Test Two | WORD LINKS | Question 89 |
| --- | --- | --- |

Link the following words together:

Cheshire, Whittington, Archer, Stilton
Mayor, Cheese, Cat, Sherwood

| Test Two | SIX VOWELS | Question 90 |
| --- | --- | --- |

Can you think of a word that contains six identical vowels?

| Test Two | ORDERED VOWELS | Question 91 |
|---|---|---|

There are also three words which contain all five vowels in the correct order. What are they?

| Test Two | REVERSED VOWELS | Question 92 |
|---|---|---|

Following on from question 91, there are also three words which feature the five vowels in reverse order. Can you think of them?

| Test Two | HEAVY BALL | Question 93 |
|---|---|---|

Given nine balls, identical except that one is slightly heavier than the rest, how can the odd one out be determined, using only two operations on a simple balancing scale?

| Test Two | CLOCK HANDS | Question 94 |
|---|---|---|

At precisely 6am the angle between the minute and hour hand of a clock is 180 degrees. To the nearest second, what time will it be when the angle between the two hands is again 180 degrees?

| Test Two | THREE PIECE SUIT | Question 95 |
|---|---|---|

If trousers and waistcoat cost £30, jacket and trousers cost £40 and waistcoat and jacket cost £32, how much is a three piece suit?

| Test Two | AND | Question 96 |
|---|---|---|

Can readers think of a type of sentence which has the word 'and' in it five times consecutively?

You are in a quiz show with a chance to win a million pounds by selecting the correct box from three. The host – and this is *very* important – knows which box contains the million. You make your choice and then the host opens one of the other boxes to reveal it as empty. He then offers you the chance to change your mind and select the remaining box. Should you do this?

Professor Muddle has mixed up his historical dates. Can you help?

1066, 753BC, 1815, 1649
Battle of Waterloo, King Charles I executed, Battle of Hastings, Foundation of Rome

Can you arrange three matchsticks of equal length to form a square?

Don Fernando, the cruelly capricious prison governor, loves to torment his charges with tantalising tricks. He places prisoners A, B and C in cell 1 and prisoners D and E in cell 2. All prisoners know he has distributed a total of three white hats and two black hats to the prisoners and the distribution is as follows: A white; B white; C black; D black; E white. The prisoners can see their fellows' hats, but not their own. The first prisoner to identify the colour of their own hat gets double rations the following week. Which prisoners are in a position to identify their own hat?

---

**DID YOU KNOW?**
More electrical impulses are generated in one day by a single human brain than by all the telephones in the world.

# TEST THREE

| Test Three | **COUNT THE DAYS** | Question 1 |
|---|---|---|

Starting on 1 Jan and ending on 31 Dec, what is the minimum number of days in ten years?

| Test Three | **REPETITION** | Question 2 |
|---|---|---|

Can you think of a sentence with the same word eleven times consecutively?

| Test Three | **SAND** | Question 3 |
|---|---|---|

If a bag of sand weighs 50 pounds divided by half its weight, how much does the bag weigh?

| Test Three | **IN TANDEM** | Question 4 |
|---|---|---|

Two people cycle round a track. One completes 16 circuits per hour and the other completes 10 circuits per hour. If they both start from the same point, how long will it be until they are together again?

| Test Three | **CRYPTIC CLUE** | Question 5 |
|---|---|---|

The letters ENTURY represent which well known saying?

| Test Three | **LONGEST MONTH** | Question 6 |
|---|---|---|

February is the shortest month, but which is the longest?

| Test Three | **SEQUENCE #11** | Question 7 |
|---|---|---|

What comes next in this sequence?

61, 52, 63, 94, 46, ??

Change SNAIL to SHELL in six steps, one letter at a time, creating a proper word at each stage.

Who is reputed to have been responsible for killing a quarter of the world's population?

82 players take part in a knockout tennis tournament. 18 first round matches reduce the field to 64 who then continue in normal knockout fashion. How many matches are played in total?

If the first thirty numbers are listed in words (i.e. one, two, three etc.), how many 'n's are there?

Which prominent cricketer has the surname of a sea spelt backwards?

The first six letters of the alphabet appear in only four words. One of these is BIFURCATED. Can you think of the other three?

Following on from question 213, there is a slightly contrived hyphenated word which contains the first seven letters. Can you think of it?

And can you find six-letter words in which the letters appear in alphabetical order?

Starting in 1948, which city follows London, Helsinki, Melbourne, Rome?

It is a perfect square, it is a three digit number. If you rotate it through 180 degrees it is also a perfect square. If you swap the last two digits it is also a perfect square. What is it?

What is the next number in this sequence?

1,485, 1,509, 1,547, 1,553, ????

It is a three digit number. It is palindromic; it is a perfect square; the sum of the digits is prime. What is it?

What is the missing number in the sequence?

??, 49, 36, 18, 8

| Test Three | ODD ONE | Question 21 |

Which of the following pair of linked words is the odd one?

bear – borne
do – done
fly – flown
mow – mown
shear – shorn

| Test Three | DIFFERENCE | Question 22 |

What is the difference between a cob and a pen?

| Test Three | EVEN DATES | Question 23 |

Wednesday 2 February 2000 can be expressed exclusively with even numbers (considering 0 to be even), e.g. 2/2/2000. When was the previous time that happened?

| Test Three | CLEVER BIRD | Question 24 |

Which bird is reputed to have the highest IQ?

| Test Three | COLLECTIVE NOUNS | Question 25 |

Flock, fleet and flight – to what do these terms refer as collective nouns?

| Test Three | BIRTHDAYS | Question 26 |

Peter and his teenage grand-daughter Gemma share the same birthday. This year it was noted that the square of Peter's age was equal to the cube of Gemma's age. How old is Peter?

| Test Three | LOCATION | Question 27 |
|---|---|---|

Positions can be defined by 3 figure bearings measured clockwise from North, e.g. East = 090. My position is 7 degrees clockwise from North. Who am I?

| Test Three | FOUR DIGITS | Question 28 |
|---|---|---|

It is a four digit number. It is a perfect square. It reads the same upside down. Its square root is a prime number. What is it?

| Test Three | STRANGE NUMBER | Question 29 |
|---|---|---|

What is very strange about the number 6,174 which makes it unique among four digit numbers? (It is to do with repeated subtractions.)

| Test Three | NEPTUNE | Question 30 |
|---|---|---|

Neptune is to Poseidon as Ceres is to ………?

| Test Three | SPECIAL LETTERS | Question 31 |
|---|---|---|

What does it take to write the following poem, and which two letters are special?

go in June dear
go pick some very small quantity of precious azure stone
and weave all together with a braid
bind fix or die

| Test Three | REVERSED SQUARE | Question 32 |
|---|---|---|

Which number when reversed and squared will give its own squared value in reverse?

'The dough-faced plough-boy coughed and hiccoughed his rough way through the borough.'
What is unusual about this sentence?

The following is a difficult question. What is the longest single word palindrome in French?
(Clue: think of commandos.)

'Doc – note, I dissent, a fast never prevents a fatness – I diet on cod.' What is unusual about this
sentence?

What is the longest word you can come up with which does not repeat any letters? There is one
that is 16 letters long.

What is the significance of the following infinitely recurring sequence?

1, 4, 9, 6, 5, 6, 9, 4, 1, 0, 1, 4, 9, 6, 5, 6, 9, 4, 1, 0 ..........

What follows next in this sequence?

QAZ, WSX, EDC, RFV, TGB, ???

| Test Three | REWRITE | Question 39 |

How could the following statement be rewritten so as to make sense?

X, Y, D, TTT and 7 all eventually end in C.

| Test Three | DAYS OLD | Question 40 |

On his birthday in 1992 Dr Primes was intrigued to note that his age in years multiplied by the day in the year (considered numerically with 1 January equalling one) came to 11,111. What was his age and date of birth?

| Test Three | LONG JOURNEY | Question 41 |

Imagine that you start a journey from a fixed point and proceed as follows: you travel 1,000 miles north, 1,000 miles east, 1,000 miles south and 1,000 miles west.

At what point must you begin your journey in order to arrive back at exactly the same point at which you departed?

| Test Three | NO WAY | Question 42 |

You are still on the journey described in question 41.

And what starting points is it impossible to complete such a journey?

**DID YOU KNOW?**
Results from cognitive tests show 30% of 80-year-olds perform as well as young adults.

What do the words 'Silver', 'Purple', 'Orange' and 'Month' have in common?

What refreshment can be made from WINTER COAT?

If I arrive at Trafalgar Square at five past six in the evening, what time do I get to Waterloo?

Give the next two terms in the following series:

a) UDTQC
b) LMMJV

The well known sentence which contains all the letters of the alphabet is 'The quick brown fox jumped over the lazy dog'. Can you think of an example only 32 letters long?

Catherine's birthday has just passed and she has given birth very recently. The year's calendar (2000) is exactly the same as the one when she was born. How old is Catherine?

| Test Three | COMMON WORDS | Question 49 |
|---|---|---|

What do the following have in common?

CALMNESS, CANOPY, DEFT, FIRST, SIGHING, STUPID

| Test Three | HEAVIER | Question 50 |
|---|---|---|

Which is heavier, an ounce of gold or an ounce of sugar?

| Test Three | REMARKABLE NUMBERS | Question 51 |
|---|---|---|

The number 153 is remarkable because 1 (raised to the 3) + 5 (raised to the 3) + 3 (raised to the 3) = 153. Why is 54,748 remarkable?

| Test Three | ANALYSE THIS | Question 52 |
|---|---|---|

Explain the following:

woo ten, true of her, if vex is, given sheet, teen inn, new velvet eel

| Test Three | SERIES #4 | Question 53 |
|---|---|---|

What comes next: F4E, S9, SE5EN?

| Test Three | CONSECUTIVE VOWELS | Question 54 |
|---|---|---|

What is the only English word which contains five consecutive vowels?

100 degrees Celsius is equivalent to 212 degrees Fahrenheit and 0 degrees Celsius is equivalent to 32 degrees Fahrenheit. What is the only temperature which is expressed in the same number of degrees on both scales?

What is your best estimate for the number of complete revolutions a 5p coin would make to roll the full width of a £20 note?

Martians need 21,300 miles of cable to lay a telephone wire around their equator. How much more cable would they need to hang the wire on six inch telegraph poles?

What is remarkable about the following equation?

11 + 2 = 12 + 1

Why do many science students find it useful to learn this sentence: 'How I like a drink, alcoholic of course, after the heavy lectures involving quantum mechanics'?

Which is the only London Underground station that does not include a letter from the word 'Mackerel'?

At the time when telephone numbers consisted of both letters and numbers why should the then Duke of Marlborough's number have been BROM4689?

If five spiders can catch five flies in five minutes.

a) How long would it take 100 spiders to catch 100 flies?
b) How many flies would 100 spiders catch in 100 minutes?

What have the occupations of blacksmith, fishmonger, lumberjack and journalist in common with my friend Mr Mackintosh?

In the armed services during World War II, Iceland was officially known as Iceland (c). Why was this a dashed good idea?

Is it more correct to say 'yolk is white' or 'yolk are white'?

Why have the following words got nothing in common?

naughtiness, senility, cloverleaf, shelducks

| Test Three | PRIME NUMBERS | Question 67 |
|---|---|---|

It is possible to make numerous nine digit numbers which comprise each of the nine digits used once each (e.g. 392874651). How many of these numbers are prime?

| Test Three | DECIPHER | Question 68 |
|---|---|---|

Can you make sense of this?

YYURYYUBICURYYIVME

| Test Three | COMMONALITY | Question 69 |
|---|---|---|

What have the following words in common?
xenophobic, weird, vile, thieving, selfish

| Test Three | PATHWAY | Question 70 |
|---|---|---|

Form a series of words from GATE to DOOR via PATH in seven moves, changing one letter per move and forming proper words at each step.

---

**DID YOU KNOW?**
An analysis of 1 million students in a New York school district showed that school cafeteria food affected IQ scores to an astonishing degree. When preservatives, coloring, dyes and artificial flavors were removed from the cafeteria menu researchers found that 70,000 students performed two or more IQ grade levels higher than before.

Can you think of two examples of nine-letter words which have a special property? The property is that you can remove one letter of the word at a time (i.e. leaving eight letters, then seven etc.) in such a way that all the remaining combinations of letters make valid words.

Following on from question 71, there are two nine-letter examples which break all the way down to a one-letter word, but only knock off letters at the beginning or end of the words. Can you find them?

When was the last year in which someone could have been born in order to live in a year which was the square of their age?

Can you make sense of this?

If the B mt put: If the B. putting:

Catherine has nine sweets and four bags. How can she distribute the sweets so that she has an odd number of sweets in each bag?

Adding your age after your year 2000 birthday to the year you were born will give the total 100. When will this next happen?

Why are September, October, November and December all two out?

Match the words in the following two collections:

Pea, Key, Sea, Swans, Whales, Locusts, Handel
Salt, Concerto, Green, Pod, Swarm, Fleet, Door

Pungent is to taste as ......... is to sound?

Is it muted, cacophonous, muffled or deafening?

In the *Paradiso*, Canto XXVIII vv 92–93, Dante wrote: 'There were so many angels that their quantity would surpass the number you would achieve by the geometrical process of doubling the chess squares.' (i.e. 1st square = 1, 2nd square = 2, 3rd square = 4 etc.). What was the number of angels?

---

**DID YOU KNOW?**
The brain weighs about the same as a bag of sugar – approximately 2% of bodyweight. But it accounts for up to 20% of the body's energy needs. Each nerve cell in the brain can be connected with up to 100,000 others. Counting each nerve connection in the human brain cortex – the outer layer – at the rate of 1 per second would take 32 million years.

| Test Three | BRICKS | Question 81 |
|---|---|---|

If a brick weighs 3 pounds plus the weight of half a brick, what does a brick and a half weigh?

| Test Three | USAGE | Question 82 |
|---|---|---|

Four uses four; five uses five; six uses six. Seven merely uses three, whereas only eight uses all seven. With this information, say how many do one and two use?

| Test Three | DOUBLE LETTERS | Question 83 |
|---|---|---|

What word contains three consecutive sets of double letters?

| Test Three | KEY | Question 84 |
|---|---|---|

What is the key to the following sequence? E T A O I N S H R D L U

| Test Three | SYLLABLES | Question 85 |
|---|---|---|

Can you think of a one syllable word that converts to a three syllable word by the insertion of only one extra letter?

| Test Three | SEQUENCE #14 | Question 86 |
|---|---|---|

What is the next number in this sequence? 1, 2, 3, 7, 22

| Test Three | FOUR-LETTER WORDS | Question 87 |
|---|---|---|

Can you find six four-letter words which use the same four letters?

After 1957 comes 1958 and then 1959. If 1960 is not next, what is?

What is the common link between these words?

house, pure, kitchen, swear, dribble, desk

In Great Britain the four seasons are of exactly the same length, but in France spring is much longer than summer, why?

Can you change the word 'rot' to 'resurrection' by adding one letter at each stage? You are allowed to make anagrams of the previous words, e.g. you can add an 'n' and make 'torn'.

Which is the next letter in the following sequence? M V E M J S U N

Which two important battles were separated by exactly 300 years?

Actually the answer to the previous question is not strictly correct. Why not?

| **Test Three** | **WILDLIFE** | **Question 95** |

What do the following have in common: the ring-tailed cat, the crayfish, the firefly, the glass snake, the horned toad and the civet cat?

| **Test Three** | **RACETRACK** | **Question 96** |

Can you name an obscure town, which used to be known for National Hunt racing, which contains half the letters of the alphabet?

| **Test Three** | **FOREIGN NUMBERS** | **Question 97** |

What do the following numbers have in common in their various languages?
four (English), vier (German), tre (Italian) and cinco (Spanish)

| **Test Three** | **PECULIAR SENTENCE** | **Question 98** |

What is peculiar about the following sentence?

'Roman court chose a coin or pain.'

| **Test Three** | **SIX-LETTER WORDS** | **Question 99** |

Can you find seven six-letter words which all use the same letters?

| **Test Three** | **PRESIDENTIAL ELECTION** | **Question 100** |

Can you change BUSH to GORE in five steps, changing one letter at a time and making valid words on the way?

# TEST FOUR

In what medium could two Es be said to make an I, two Is be said to make an H, and two Ts be said to make an M?

Which is the next number in the series?

2, 4, 6, 30, 32, 34, 36, 40, 42, 44, 46, 50, 52, 54, 56, 60, 62, 64, 66, ?

In a DIY store I can buy one for £1, ten for £2 and one hundred for £3. What are they?

Can you think of a nine-letter word which has the same vowel five times plus four consonants?

What is peculiar about the following pious hope?

'May the sin of usury not win rewards.'

On an ordinary analogue watch or clock face, how many times will the minute hand pass completely over the hour hand in twelve hours, starting at 12 noon?

Can you think of a 13-letter word which features the same vowel four times and has only three other consonants?

Match the following five words:

       stone, part, brim, nut, cross

with these:

       ridge, bill, chat, hatch, stone

and then decide which combination is the odd one out.

Most nouns in the English language are pluralised by the addition of an 's'. Can you find a common word, that with the addition of an 's' is not only turned from a plural into a singular, but also changes gender?

What do the following have in common?

bg, dn, ht, pp, pt, tn

Form words from each of the following by inserting six consonants and a hyphen:

SI\*\*\*\*\*\*EEN, CA\*\*\*\*\*\*ASE, WA\*\*\*\*\*\*AP

| Test Four | APPEARANCES | Question 12 |
|---|---|---|

Can you think of two English words that look like opposites but actually have the same meaning?

| Test Four | FROM A TO B | Question 13 |
|---|---|---|

It takes three days to go from A to B, but four days to go from B to A. Name A and B.

| Test Four | ABBREVIATION | Question 14 |
|---|---|---|

What well known abbreviation, when spoken, uses twice as many syllables as the three words it stands for?

| Test Four | TIMEPIECE | Question 15 |
|---|---|---|

Which timepiece has the greatest number of moving parts?

| Test Four | RESOLUTIONS | Question 16 |
|---|---|---|

What New Year resolution is impossible to keep and yet also impossible to break?

| Test Four | THE KNOWLEDGE | Question 17 |
|---|---|---|

Can you think of a well known London thoroughfare of 13 letters which has only three vowels?

| Test Four | ONE AND A HALF | Question 18 |
|---|---|---|

Simon is one and a half times as old as Niall, who is one and a half times as old as David. Their ages total 152 years. How old is Niall?

| Test Four | TRANSLATE | Question 19 |
|---|---|---|

Can you make sense of this:

'Oyo is an imyant y in Yugal which exys y.'

| Test Four | COMMON THEME | Question 20 |
|---|---|---|

What do the following words have in common?

hand, point, foot, water

| Test Four | COMPLETION | Question 21 |
|---|---|---|

The sequence plead, label, album, lusty, ????? is completed by which of the following words?

frown, lunch, until, launch

| Test Four | SPECIAL DAY | Question 22 |
|---|---|---|

Dates can be represented in several ways using three numbers, e.g. 24 March 2001 can be written as 2431, 240301, 1324 or 010324. Using all four methods what makes 4th April 2001 a special day?

| Test Four | UNUSUAL LETTERS | Question 23 |
|---|---|---|

What's so very unusual about the letters in the words LIMNOPHILOUS (living in ponds or marshes) and UNDERSTUDY?

What do the following words have in common?

herd, sent, sty, rein, our, new, by, rest

How can tin, oxygen and tungsten make the weather colder?

What kind of bathroom might the following numbers suggest to a Frenchman: 11, 8?

Put the following together:

Columbus, Marlowe, Goethe, Gutenberg, da Vinci

Mona Lisa, Bible, America, Faust, Tamberlaine

100 crows are perched at evenly spaced intervals on a telegraph wire. Ted, Joe and Dan fire simultaneously at the crows. Ted kills all the crows on the first one fifth of the wire, Joe kills 10% of the remainder, while Dan kills all birds on 20% of the length of the wire. How many birds remain on the wire?

The word 'reviver' is a palindrome, i.e. reads the same forwards as backwards. Can you think of a seven-letter palindrome which contains four vowels?

The letters A, H, I, M and O are reversible in that they are unaltered if viewed from behind. In what context are D, N, R and U the only reversible letters?

Both Margaret Thatcher and Ronald Reagan suffer from the medical condition Dupuytren's Contracture. (This causes clawing of the fingers and affects the ability to type.) What is unusual about Dupuytren's Contracture?

I am reclining on a lilo, alone in a swimming pool. I am holding a brick on my lap which I then release into the water where it obviously sinks to the bottom. Does the water level in the pool rise slightly, stay the same or go down slightly?

Identify the following and connect them:

a) A unit of pressure
b) A Manchester United hero in Barcelona
c) A palindromic woman
d) A 'satisfactory' GCSE 'pass'
e) A Shakespearean king

If you were milking a cow, how far away would you be from the nearest religious book?

If R = 80, C = 100 and K = 373, what is the value of F?

A farmer died leaving three sons. He bequeathed the first son half of his cattle, the second one-third and to the third son one-ninth. He had 17 cows in total. How did they solve the problem of dividing up the cattle?

Two fathers and two sons leave a town. The population only goes down by three. Why?

Alan needs to some Bill some important documents which must be secured in a chest with a padlock. However, the courier company is unreliable and will steal anything that is not in a locked chest (e.g. a key sent separately will be stolen). Alan has various padlocks and keys, as does Bill. How can they coordinate to transfer the documents safely?

A ship leaves a dock, and travels right around the world arriving back at its original starting place exactly. In exactly the same place it started from. Which part of the ship travelled the furthest?

A young oak tree had ten branches. In May each branch grew 60 leaves. Each of the following months it grew 10 more leaves on each branch. How many leaves would it have seven months later?

A man pushes his car along until he stops in front of a hotel. He suddenly realises that he is bankrupt. How can this be?

Make the longest word you can from the letters N, A, S, I, T, E. You can't use any letter twice.

A drinks machine has three options: tea, coffee and random. A friend tells you that the machine is faulty and that the buttons are never correct. Each drink is 50p. How much money would you need to spend to know which buttons deliver which drinks?

It's breakfast time and you need to boil an egg. It must be boiled for nine minutes and you have only a 4 minute and a 7 minute egg timer. How can you do the egg?

A man is wearing a suit and one glove. He is dead, why?

A man goes into a baker's shop and puts 50p on the counter. 'Brown or white?' asks the shop assistant. Later that day another man comes in and again puts 50p on the counter. This time the shop assistant knows for sure that he wants a brown loaf. How?

Equal weights are dropped simultaneously from the same height into buckets on the ground. The first has 4 inches of water at 40 degrees Fahrenheit and the second has 3 inches of water at 30 degrees Fahrenheit. Which reaches the bottom of the bucket first?

In a balloon, stationary off the coast of Ireland, I dropped two wine bottles off the side. If one was full, and the other was empty, which hit the ground first?

Lenny has just parked in a car park and needs to remember the location. The spaces to the left read 16, 06, 68, 88 and the one on the right is 98. What number did he park his car?

Why is Jason not a man for all seasons?

Which seven-letter word starts masculine, changes to feminine, then back to masculine and ends up feminine?

A woman catches the train to go shopping each week. She can go to Eastlea or Westlea and doesn't mind which. Trains for both destinations arrive every ten minutes and she always catches the first available train. Why does she end up in Westlea nine weeks out of ten?

Which ten-letter word can be composed using only the first line of letters on a keyboard (QWERTYUIOP) ?

In chess, there is one specific type of move which the queen is unable to make, but all the other pieces can. What is it?

If ANTE minus ETNA equals NEAT (all four-digit numbers), what digits are represented by A, N, T and E?

**DID YOU KNOW?**
The IQ test was originated by Alfred Binet (1857–1911) as an objective measure of comprehension, reasoning and judgement. Binet was motivated by a powerful enthusiasm for the emerging discipline of psychology and a desire to overcome the cultural and class prejudices of late 19th century France in the assessment of children's academic potential.

A shoe box measures $10 \times 4 \times 4$ inches. A fly is sitting centrally on the top of one end, while a spider is waiting opposite, on the bottom, at the other end. What distance must the spider cover to catch the fly?

John took some coins from his money box and arranged them in the following way:

£2, 50p, 2p, £1, 20p, 1p, 5p

Why?

Why is the sum £8.88 special?

John is an old age pensioner. Reversing the digits of his age this year and doubling the answer gives his age next year. How old is John?

In the following, each capital letter has a consistent value. Can you work them out?

[KEENE + BRAIN] × 4 = WEEKLY

**PUNCH THE CLOCK**

A clock strikes the hour every hour and also strikes just once every 15 minutes. If you can only hear the clock what is the longest time you can wait before being completely certain what the correct time is?

**SHAPES AND COLOURS**

How are a red triangle, a purple square, an orange diamond and a green circle related?

**EQUATE THIS**

How can the following be made true with the addition of one line?

5 + 5 + 5 = 550

**SQUARE AGES**

This year my father's age, my son's age and my daughter's age are all square numbers. When my daughter was born, my age was also a square number and exactly the same as my father's age when I was born. How old am I now?

**SERIES #6**

The following is part of a commonly encountered series of digits: 10111212. What immediately precedes it?

**HOCUS POCUS**

What do the letters represent in the following addition?

HOCUS + POCUS = PRESTO.

A train is travelling at 100 miles per hour. There is a spot of oil on one wheel. What speed is this spot doing, in relation to the ground, when it reaches its highest point?

Can you think of four English words which are pronounced the same but all spelt differently?

Can you think of a pair of English words that are pronounced the same but are spelled using entirely different letters?

Can you think of a pair of English words which are spelt differently, but sound the same and have the same meaning?

What is the next number in this sequence?

1, 8, 11, 69, 88, 96

Explain these five numbers:

1, 5, 9, 15, 21

Explain the following pairings:

(1,3), (2,3), (3,5), (4,4), (5,4), (6,3), (7,5), (8,5), (9,4), (10,3)

What is remarkable about the following sentence?

'The picture shows an English woman and two Asian women at work in a crowded North London shop.'

What is the next number in this series?

13, 44, 88, 176, 847, ???

Can you think of any English words that can have two different, entirely opposite meanings?

What is unusual about multiples of the number 142,857?

Can you think of three examples of pairs of five letter English words which are anagrams of each other and sound the same?

If 44 + 7 = RUN and 6 + 85 = CAT and 5 + 76 + 16 = BOSS, what does 35 + 33 + 16 equal?

Imagine a four-by-four grid consisting of 16 squares. How many rectangles (including squares) of any size, does this contain?

Where could you observe that:

1 = 2, 2 = 5, 3 = 5, 4 = 4, 5 = 5, 6 = 5, 7 = 3, 8 = 7 and 9 = 5 ?

What are the next two in the following sequence: 95:E L5:E 85:E ?

What is the significance of the following dates in any non-leap year: 10 April, 19 July, 27 October?

What do the following words have in common?

Deer, Dress, Look, Poll, Sew, Tresses, Was

| Test Four | EQUAL AND OPPOSITE | Question 85 |

Can you think of two adjectives with opposite meanings, which, when used as verbs, mean the same thing?

| Test Four | NO EIGHT | Question 86 |

Why is the following number interesting? (Clue: multiplication is the key.)

12345679

| Test Four | REVERSED RHYME | Question 87 |

Can you think of a word of three letters (all different) which, when reversed, provides another word, rhyming with the original?

| Test Four | NOT OUT | Question 88 |

In a cricket match, each batsman is bowled out first ball. Who is the remaining not out batsman?

| Test Four | SERIES #8 | Question 89 |

What are the next two letters in this series?

F, S, T, F, F, S, S, ?, ?

| Test Four | DIGITAL CLOCK | Question 90 |

Imagine a digital clock where you can only see the bottom three segments, as the upper four are obscured. For a 12-hour clock, what are the only times which can be read with no ambiguity?

Which word is this?

'Alone, I am cold. I become hot if you add the letter 'i' to me, but I turn cold again if you add 'y' instead.'

What word uses over 50 per cent of the letters of the alphabet once and once only?

In which medium could it be said that ONE = 6666633, SIX = 777744499 and FORTY = 3336667778999?

What remarkable event happened in the evening on the third Wednesday in February 2002?

Using the numbers 1 to 9 in order and using only normal mathematical signs (add, subtract, multiply, divide and brackets) create an equation which sums to 100.

Name three units of measurement which sound like three consecutive letters of the alphabet.

In the equation $A \times B = C$, the ten digits 0–9 are used once each. Can you construct the equation?

Can you punctuate the following sentence so that it makes sense?

time flies you cannot their flight is too erratic

Each digit display on the panel of a mechanical, digital, 24-hour, railway station clock has the standard seven segments. At what time does the greatest number movements occur?

Where might a prayer follow White Dogwood, Golden Bell, and Azalea?

# TEST FIVE

| Test Five | INFLATION | Question 1 |
|---|---|---|

Why are 1997 50p coins worth more than 1996 50p coins?

| Test Five | NUMERICAL PROPERTY | Question 2 |
|---|---|---|

The numbers 3, 7, 8, 40, 50 and 60 have a property in common which no other number has. What is that property?

| Test Five | COUNTING IN FRENCH | Question 3 |
|---|---|---|

What comes next in this sequence?

un, deux, quatre, six, trois

| Test Five | PUZZLING WORDS | Question 4 |
|---|---|---|

I have two five-letter words. I take the first letter of one and put it at the front of the other to make a four-letter and a six-letter word. The meaning of the four-letter word has not changed, but the six-letter word now means the opposite of its original. What are the original two words?

| Test Five | OXYGEN | Question 5 |
|---|---|---|

As altitude increases what happens to the ratio of oxygen in the air?

a) It gets less and it becomes more difficult to breathe.
b) It increases.
c) It remains the same.

| Test Five | IN THE CHAIR | Question 6 |
|---|---|---|

When you enter the Cabinet Room at 10 Downing Street how would you differentiate the chair of the Prime Minister from those of the ministers?

| Test Five | THE LETTER X | Question 7 |
|---|---|---|

Into which group of letters – and why – does the letter X go?

ABDFGHLQRT                    CKOPSUVW

| Test Five | HAVE WHAT? | Question 8 |
|---|---|---|

Two have only one, four have two, nine have three and eleven have four. What does this refer to?

| Test Five | INSIDER DEALING | Question 9 |
|---|---|---|

Two words are spelt differently but pronounced the same and you may well find some of one inside the other. What are they?

| Test Five | INSIDE AND UNDER | Question 10 |
|---|---|---|

Two words are spelt and pronounced the same and you may well find some of one inside the other? What are they?

| Test Five | THAT IS | Question 11 |
|---|---|---|

Punctuate the following sentence to make sense:

that that is is that that is not is not is that it it is

Alone I am hot. Take two letters away and I am cold. Take another away and I warm up a bit.

What am I?

Add a three-letter sequence (identical for each example, although different in each case) to the beginning and end of the following to make complete words:

\*\*\*MEN\*\*\*
\*\*\*ICEM\*\*\*
\*\*\*ERGRO\*\*

Name an African country which is an anagram of a South American capital city.

What is the longest English word which has its letters in alphabetical order?

Can you think of an eight-letter word which consists of five syllables?

Suddenly I spotted an IXAT following me. Where was I?

| Test Five | MISSING LETTER | Question 18 |
|---|---|---|

What is the missing letter?

A, F, H, K, ?, Y, Z

| Test Five | MISSING NUMBER | Question 19 |
|---|---|---|

What is the missing number in this series?

5, 8, 3, ?, 2, 1

| Test Five | BST | Question 20 |
|---|---|---|

When British Summer Time started this year I had to adjust all my timepieces. Although I did most of them around midnight, I had to leave one until after breakfast the next morning. Why?

| Test Five | TOTAL DIGITS | Question 21 |
|---|---|---|

If you write down all the possible numbers produced by the five digits 1, 3, 5, 7, 9 and then add them up, what is the total?

| Test Five | MULTIPLICATION | Question 22 |
|---|---|---|

How many terms do you get when you multiply out the following?

$(x - a)(x - b)(x - c)...(x - y)(x - z)$

| Test Five | CONSONANT STRING | Question 23 |
|---|---|---|

Which common English word contains the sequence 'tchst'? Which English place name contains the sequence 'ghtsbr'?

Which English word contains the sequence 'hh'?

What word, by the insertion of one consonant, changes its meaning from exercise power to abrogate power?

What word changes its meaning from 'approximately' to 'exactly' when you separate its first two letters?

Which historic British county is spelt with three identical letters in sequence?

The meaning of two very common verbs can be converted to their exact opposites by substituting one vowel for another. What are they?

Can you complete this three by three square so that each column, row and diagonal totals 111?

```
x 1 x
x x x
x x x
```

| Test Five | **ANCIENT GREEK** | Question 30 |
|---|---|---|

An ancient Greek lived one-fourth of his life as a boy, one-fifth as a youth, one-third as a man and spent the last 13 years of his life as an elderly gent. How old was he when he died?

| Test Five | **ODOMETER** | Question 31 |
|---|---|---|

While driving his car, Bob notes that the reading on the odometer is a palindrome – 13,931 miles. Two hours later, he notices that the new reading is another palindrome. What is the most likely speed at which he has been travelling?

| Test Five | **HYPHENATION** | Question 32 |
|---|---|---|

What word changes its meaning from 'to be kept for use ahead of other people' to 'to be kept for use after other people' by inserting a hyphen?

| Test Five | **RISK OR REWARD** | Question 33 |
|---|---|---|

What eight-letter word can mean a penalty or a reward?

| Test Five | **ODD AND EVEN** | Question 34 |
|---|---|---|

Which two odd numbers, when multiplied together, give a statement of an even number?

| Test Five | **EMOTIONS** | Question 35 |
|---|---|---|

Can you think of two words which both involve emotion? With the first, adding one letter at the end changes it from a noun to an adjective. With the second adding the same letter at the end changes it from an adjective to a noun.

| Test Five | SCOTLAND | Question 36 |
|---|---|---|

Wales has 15, Ireland has 7, England has 4. How many does Scotland have?

| Test Five | FLOREAL AND NIVOSE | Question 37 |
|---|---|---|

If Floreal is the second and Nivose is the seventh, what are the fourth and sixth?

| Test Five | WATCHING | Question 38 |
|---|---|---|

If you can see a knob, dopping, siege, sute and rush, what are you looking at?

| Test Five | EDIBLE VOWELS | Question 39 |
|---|---|---|

Can you think of a word which can be changed into its opposite by the addition of a vowel in the middle?

(Clue: think of food.)

| Test Five | HALF | Question 40 |
|---|---|---|

If a man and a half build a house and a half in a year and a half, how long does it take one man to build one house?

| Test Five | INSERTION | Question 41 |
|---|---|---|

Place the remaining numbers 8 and 9 into one or other of the two lines below:

a) 1 2 4
b) 3 5 6 7

What common word can lose either of its first two letters making three words with identical pronunciation?

Which two words are synonyms when applied to a person's career, but are antonyms when applied to his character?

How can you use the numbers 1, 3, 4 and 6 exactly once each, with the standard arithmetic operators (brackets, add, subtract, divide and multiply), to reach a total of 24?

Where, in everyday life do you find the phrase 'Standing on the shoulders of giants'?

Can you name a foodstuff that becomes uneatable if you remove a consonant?

In a room there is a man and a woman. The man's mother-in-law and the woman's mother-in-law are mother and daughter. What is the man's relationship to the woman?

| Test Five | WINE | Question 48 |
| --- | --- | --- |

You have two glasses of wine, one white, one red. You stir a spoonful of the red into the white and then a spoonful of the white into the red. Which wine is now more polluted?

| Test Five | UNRHYMING COUPLETS | Question 49 |
| --- | --- | --- |

Can you think of two words that do not rhyme and yet end in the same eight letters?

| Test Five | TWO MORE | Question 50 |
| --- | --- | --- |

Name another two words which do not rhyme despite ending in the same six letters.

| Test Five | ODD ONE OUT | Question 51 |
| --- | --- | --- |

Which of these is the odd one out?        2/2, 4/4, 6/6, 8/8, 10/10, 12/12

| Test Five | SINGLE STATE | Question 52 |
| --- | --- | --- |

Can you name, preferably without consulting a map, the only US state which has a single syllable name?

| Test Five | CITIES | Question 53 |
| --- | --- | --- |

In which city will you find truth and in which city will you find falsehood?

| Test Five | GIRLFRIEND | Question 54 |
| --- | --- | --- |

Bill said to his new girlfriend, 'Is one hug enough?' and she replied, 'Yes.' Why?

Find a four-word phrase, meaning just in time, where the last letter of the first word is the same as the first letter of the second word, with this pattern being repeated throughout the phrase.

The equation 123456789 = 100 is obviously wrong. Can you correct it by the addition of just three plus (+) or minus (−) signs between the digits on the left, keeping their order the same?

Can you think of a tree, the name of which contains all five vowels?

What is the next number in this sequence?

61, 52, 63, 94, 64, ??

---

**DID YOU KNOW?**

In April 1847, Johann Martin Dase was reported as having achieved the following calculations: multiplying two 20-digit numbers in six minutes, two 48-digit numbers in 40 minutes and, incredibly, two 100-digit numbers together in 8¾ hours (all these calculations performed mentally). Additionally, 2 × 8-digit numbers: 49,735,827 × 98,536,474 in one minute and seven seconds on paper. (Answer: 4,900,793,024,053,998). However, mentally he was even quicker with: 79,532,853 × 93,758,479 in 54 seconds. (Answer: 7,456,879,327,810,587.)

Can you find words meaning: big, kingly, a drink, a hateful look and a composer, which are all anagrams of each other?

Can you fill in the blanks in this multiplication?

$ABCD \times E = FGHI7$

The letters represent all the digits bar 7.

What do the following words have in common?

axe, defence, speciality, draught, moult, vice, colour

Of the 50 states of the USA, which of them has the most northerly, southerly, easterly and westerly territory?

Using the figures 9999 and as many mathematical symbols as you like, can you make 100?

Forwards, it's heavy, backwards, it's not. What is it?

| Test Five | **NINE ANAGRAMS** | Question 65 |
|---|---|---|

Can you think of a collection of five letters which can make nine different words, all anagrams of each other?

| Test Five | **FIVE ANAGRAMS** | Question 66 |
|---|---|---|

Things; little things; a newspaper; gives out; to strike. Can you find five five-letter anagrams?

| Test Five | **ABC** | Question 67 |
|---|---|---|

'A', 'B' and 'C' are three four-letter words. A and B have the same letters in reverse order (like mart and tram). AC is an eight-letter word which is a cryptic clue for B. CB is an 8-letter word and a cryptic clue for A. What are the words?

| Test Five | **SEQUENCE #19** | Question 68 |
|---|---|---|

Which is missing in the following sequence and why?

10, 11, 12, 13, 14, 15, 16, 17, 20, 22, 24, 31, 100, ?, 10000, 1111111111111111

| Test Five | **SEPTEMBER 1753** | Question 69 |
|---|---|---|

What happened in England between the 3rd and the 13th of September 1753?

| Test Five | **CRYPTIC ANAGRAMS** | Question 70 |
|---|---|---|

A poet steals a girl's meat and fish. Can you write a six-word sentence to this effect which contains five words which are all anagrams of each other?

| Test Five | GENERAL INCREASE | Question 71 |

What has, in general, increased from 405 to 625 since the 1960s?

| Test Five | THINKING | Question 72 |

Can you change the word THINK to BRAIN in seven steps, by changing one letter at a time and forming a proper word at each stage?

| Test Five | THREE LETTERS | Question 73 |

Can you find words which contain the following letter sequences?

XYG, XOP, WKW, YZY

| Test Five | SEQUENTIAL TIMES | Question 74 |

23 minutes past one, 26 minutes to one ...

What is the next and final item in this sequence?

| Test Five | MONKS | Question 75 |

What is the collective noun for monks?

| Test Five | UNIQUE NUMBER | Question 76 |

How is the number 40 unique?

(Clue: it is not a mathematical property.)

| Test Five | **COMMON PLACE NAMES** | Question 77 |

Apart from being place names. What else do the following have in common?

Salisbury, Newcastle, Liverpool, Derby, Aberdeen

| Test Five | **MINUTE HAND** | Question 78 |

Between now and the same time tomorrow how many times will the minute hand pass the hour hand?

| Test Five | **ANOTHER UNIQUE NUMBER** | Question 79 |

Why is the number 8,549,017,632 unique?

| Test Five | **COMPOSITE** | Question 80 |

Can you think of a two syllable word, composed of a verb and a noun, the latter seeming to contradict the meaning of the whole?

| Test Five | **SEQUENCE #20** | Question 81 |

What number is next in the following sequence?

4, 6, 2, 4, 2, 3, 9, ?

| Test Five | **EMPHASIS** | Question 82 |

What is common to the following words?

produce, import, attribute, rebel, conduct

Can you think of two ten-letter English place names which each feature the same letter used five times? (The actual letter is not the same in both cases.)

Can you think of an ancient Greek whose name consists of three successive palindromes?

Using only one arithmetical sign, complete the following equation correctly.

10 10 10 = 9.50

Can you change DRINK to CRASH in seven steps, changing one letter at a time and making correct words all along?

What seven-digit number can you enter into a calculator, turn the calculator upside-down and the display then shows a word meaning 'pursuits'?

Which commonly used, everyday word with a total of eleven letters, contains two 'D's, 2 'R's, 2 'N's and 2 'U's ?

Can you find an anagram of 'Mediterranean Boys Know'?

Pick the odd one out in the following words or phrases:

'Word', 'Noun', 'TLA', 'Verb', 'Not a sentence' (Note: TLA stands for three letter acronym.)

What is the next number in the following sequence?

2, 5, 5, 4, 5, 6, 3, 7, ?

What do the following have in common?

gold, iron, lead, mercury, potassium, silver

What is the sinister link between typists and stewardesses?

What do these words have in common?

bouquet, charm, kettle, parliament, raft, wedge

What comes next in this sequence?

1, 2, 3, 2, 1, 2, 3, 4, 2, 1, ??

What are the next two terms of the sequence

1, 2, 6, 12, 60, 60, 420, 840, ??, ??

What eight-digit number can you enter into a calculator, turn the calculator upside-down and the display then shows two words naming a multinational company?

Add two Es to the word FAR to make another English word.

What do the following words have in common?

berate, medallion, scatter, passing, canape

Insert one letter somewhere in the middle of the following words to obtain a logical collection.

coin, peer, lace, bran, jams

# TEST SIX

| Test Six | **SAIL AWAY** | **Question 1** |
|---|---|---|

How far is the North Sea from the Southern Sea?

| Test Six | **ODD WORD OUT** | **Question 2** |
|---|---|---|

Lenin, Marxist, Cenotaph, Weightless, Blowtorch, Netsuke

Numerically speaking, which is the odd one out?

| Test Six | **FIVE FROM NINE** | **Question 3** |
|---|---|---|

The following constitute five from a total of nine. What are they?

thrones, dominions, virtues, powers and principalities

| Test Six | **AND THE REST...?** | **Question 4** |
|---|---|---|

Test Six from Question 503, what are the other four? Followingn

| Test Six | **UNCHANGED MEANING** | **Question 5** |
|---|---|---|

Take an English concrete noun of three letters. Invert it and double the last (previously first) letter. Surprisingly, you haven't changed the meaning. What are the words?

| Test Six | **FAKE?** | **Question 6** |
|---|---|---|

If you find a coin dated 55BC how can you tell whether it is a fake?

| Test Six | END OF THE ALPHABET | Question 7 |

If A = 1, B = 2, C = 3 etc, then can you find a six-letter word that adds up to 127?

| Test Six | DAVID IN THE MIDDLE | Question 8 |

David is bigger than Maude, but smaller than Lupe. What do these refer to?

| Test Six | UNIQUE 1666 | Question 9 |

What is mathematically interesting and unique about the year 1666?

| Test Six | ANOTHER LETTER | Question 10 |

Which of the following is the odd one out?

arson, each, honey, inch, latitude, melon, odium, reach, salter, urge

(Clue: The answer involves another letter which does not occur in any of these words.)

| Test Six | PALINDROMIC LANGUAGE | Question 11 |

The name of the spoken and written language of which state is a palindrome?

| Test Six | ODD PLACE | Question 12 |

Which of the following is the odd one out?

Adelaide, Bruges, Cairo, Calgary, Ely, Honolulu, Seville, Stirling, Stockholm

Which is the only English word with the letters GNT appearing in it in succession?

If $A - Y - X = God$

What is A?

Where might you hear this sequence?

sank, cease, set, wheat

A pair of synonyms are given the same suffix to become antonyms. What are the words?

Which is the odd one out?

Gorillas, Monkeys, Birds, Eagles, Beetles.

What is the only word in the English language which has within it the sequence TC, where TC is not followed by H?

Which two parts of the anatomy, together as a pair, will always raise a cheer?

Can you find a sequence of 100 consecutive integers, none of which contain the letter 'a'?

Can you think of two titles of Shakespeare plays which begin and end with the same letter – this letter being a vowel (thus ruling out the 'Henry's')

Who is the odd one out?

Leonardo da Vinci, Winston Churchill, John F Kennedy, John Lennon

(Clue: posthumous achievement.)

The UK has one and the USA has the other, but France has both. What?

If South Africa has six, South Korea four, Belgium three and the UK two, what does, uniquely, Libya have?

Decipher this sentence:

He spoke from 22222222222 people.

God never sees one. A king or queen rarely sees one. We see one every day. What is it?

When would you press 'START' in order to finish?

A builder has to put the numbers on 100 houses, numbered 1 to 100
How many number 9s will he need?

What, linguistically, do the colours orange, silver and purple have in common?

---

**DID YOU KNOW?**
How much does human brain think? 70,000 is the number of thoughts that it is estimated the human brain produces on an average day.

---

| Test Six | **CAPPED** | **Question 30** |
|---|---|---|

When and why are common words spelt throughout in capitals, e.g. SUPERB or SPLENDID?

| Test Six | **PERFECT SYMMETRY** | **Question 31** |
|---|---|---|

Which common three-letter word, when in capitals has perfect vertical symmetry and when in lower case (without serifs) has perfect horizontal symmetry?

| Test Six | **YUMMY QUEUE** | **Question 32** |
|---|---|---|

What is unique about the word oppositionists?

(Clue: queue and yummy have a similar property.)

| Test Six | **AFRAID OF SEX?** | **Question 33** |
|---|---|---|

What usually comes between fear and sex?

| Test Six | **GRANDAD'S MATCH** | **Question 34** |
|---|---|---|

Granddad has to light his pipe, a candle, a gas ring and a coal fire. He has only one match. What does he light first?

| Test Six | **WARNING SIGN** | **Question 35** |
|---|---|---|

What does it mean when you see this warning sign: MO7S?

Which is the odd one out?

Kat, Kai, Kir, Kefir, Krug

Can you find nine six-letter words composed of the same six letters?

In what context is 3 twice as big as 4, and 4 twice as big as 5?

Which number completes this series?

5, 1, 20, 100, 10, 2, 50, ??

Which letter is missing in this sequence?

H H E L I B E B C N O ? N E

What ???? completes the following?

ngr, Cvtsnss, nvy, ????, Lst, Prd, Slth

| Test Six | CONNECTED WORDS | Question 42 |
|---|---|---|

What is the connection between the following?

cur, nu, ear, mar, pit, turn, ran, tun, to

| Test Six | AMERICAN CHEMISTRY | Question 43 |
|---|---|---|

The following US states are linked to chemistry in a specific way. All, except one. Which one and why?

Alabama, Arkansas, California, Georgia, Kentucky, Minnesota, Missouri, Nebraska, Pennsylvania

| Test Six | FINAL ELEMENT | Question 44 |
|---|---|---|

What is the final element of this series?

calm, breeze, gale, storm, ?????

| Test Six | CHRONOLOGICAL | Question 45 |
|---|---|---|

Which four consecutive letters of the alphabet can be rearranged in a chronological order?

| Test Six | LINKED WORDS | Question 46 |
|---|---|---|

What links the following words?

Indolent, Appropriate, Utilise

What word is suggested by the following series of numbers?

100015050

Can you think of a nine-letter word which consists of a vowel followed by eight consonants?

The standard calendar comprises 4 seasons, 13 lunar months, 52 weeks and 364 + 1 days. For what other group do these numbers provide a good fit?

What do the following letters have in common?

g, k, m, p, w

What do the following have in common?

DVA, DEUX, ZWEI, DUE, DOS

Which single word links Austrian composer Joseph Haydn, English writer Ben Jonson, and American actor Robert Trebor?

What pair of letters comes next?

ST, ND, RD, TH, ??

Add two letters to a common four-letter verb to get a six-letter noun. The noun can be both subject and object of the verb. What is the verb?

What can you do with the second word in each of these couplets that you can't do with the first?

earned/learned, low/sow, dead/read, mouse/house

Can you decipher these words?

IDER, CARIIN, IVGOX, GRVIII.

Which of the following is the odd one out?

boson, electron, fermion, muon, pion, prion, positron

What do the following words have in common?

arty, excel, geodesy, queue, any, Vienna

What number comes next in the series below, and what is the connection with bees?

1, 7, 19, 37, 61, 91, ??

With two sand-filled timers, one of 5 minutes, one of 7 minutes, how do you measure 13 minutes, without wasting any time?

What is the 2-digit decimal number that becomes its hexadecimal equivalent when the order of the digits is reversed?

Which of these is the odd one out?

hijack, defend, porter, abcess, stupid

Why, in terms of modern technology, are the latters 's' and 'z' odd ones out?

Which are the two terms missing from this sequence?

Brilliant, diamond, pearl, ruby, nonpareil, emerald, minion, brevier, bourgeois, long primer, ?, ?, English, Great Primer, Paragon

Which worker in the countryside needs to know about crooks and theaves?

Which worker in the town needs to know about fettling and nibbling?

Can you think of a girl's name of four letters, which has five anagrams?

What is the next number in this series?

1, 10, 11, 100, 101, ??

What have the following in common?

Volkswagen, opus, compact disc, saint, number

What have the following in common?

Hearts, beds, oxen, knots, links.

What connects the following?

BC, BCE, AD, CE

The following is part of a commonly encountered series of digits: 10111212. What immediately precedes it?

In a sporting context, taking the sequence – X, 2, 3, 4, 5, 6, 7, Y – where would you find that X does not equal 1 and Y does not equal 8?

In science, which particle is half of the alphabet?

Which anatomical feature might exhibit the following?

arch, double loop, radial loop, tented loop, lunar loop, whorl

| Test Six | MUSICAL POSSESSION | Question 76 |

What does someone playing a cello, a violin, or a cymbal have, that someone playing a trumpet, a fiddle, or a drum not have?

| Test Six | FIVE WORDS | Question 77 |

Can you make five English words from Roman numerals?

| Test Six | COMMON PLACE NAMES | Question 78 |

What do these five places have in common?

Athens, Madrid, N'Djamena, Vientiane, Paris

| Test Six | SEQUENCE KEY | Question 79 |

What is the key behind the following sequence of numbers 1–10?

8, 5, 4, 9, 1, 7, 6, 10, 3, 2

| Test Six | EATS, SHOOTS AND LEAVES | Question 80 |

Grammatically speaking, what is uniquely wrong with the sentence:

'The blond girl was really a brunette.'

| Test Six | COMMON WORDS | Question 81 |

What do these words have in common?

cleanse, whinge, trail, crude, broil

Which of the following is the odd one out (the blank is deliberate)?

CHI, RO, , WIN, BAR, MAN

(Clue: think of UK place names.)

What is the key to the following list?

Denmark, Sweden, UK – 0
Australia, France – 1
Canada, Cyprus – 2
Belgium – 3
Switzerland – 4
South Africa – 11

Which British public school might be represented as 5–14?

The systematic transliteration of the letters in HOCUS POCUS (i.e. both 'O's are replaced with the same new letter, as are all the others), produces a new term of similar meaning. What is it?

What have the following in common?

retinol, thiamine, ascorbic acid, calciferol, tocopherol

The following are all types of what?

comminuted, impacted, green-stick, simple

Given six matchsticks, how can you arrange them to form four identical equilateral triangles?

Which of the following is the odd one out?

koruna, kroon, krone, kudos, kuna, kwanze, kyat

What is missing from the following list?

Phalanges, metatarsus, tarsus, fibula and tibia, ??, femur, pelvis

What word can be placed in front of all of the following?

**** Terrier, **** Crab, **** Lincs, **** Strangler, **** Mass,

Under what heading might the following be grouped?

Dull, Elbow, Pinch, Rugby, Shadow, Silence

If MALE can be extracted from MASCULINE, what shorter synonyms can be extracted from the following words?

appropriate, fairy, indolent, latest, market, renegate, rogue, routine, salvage

Which same three letters can be added to each end of, 'ergro', to make them below?

What do these words have in common: bed, buck, staff, wilt?

What do these words have in common: cheese, fish, iron, war?

Which is the odd one out in this list?

bard, clef, door, flog, gnat, liar, laid, spit, tort

Which is the odd one out in this list?

desert, does, invalid, live, quest, sow, tear

On a ship what goes from bow to stern on the port side and from stern to bow on the starboard side?

How can $5/12 = 12/5$?

---

**DID YOU KNOW?**

A study published in the January 2009 edition of *Hippocampus* finds that older adults (59 to 81 years) who were more fit had increased spatial memory compared to less fit adults of the same age. They also had a bigger part of the brain, called the hippocampus, which is involved in learning and memory.

# TEST SEVEN

| Test Seven | SIXES AND NINES | Question 1 |

A builder has to buy numbers for 100 houses. The 6s and 9s are reversible. Which costs less, to buy all 9s or all 6s?

| Test Seven | LONGEST MONTH | Question 2 |

February is the shortest month, but which is the longest?

| Test Seven | ODD ONE OUT | Question 3 |

Which of the following is the odd one out?

active, comprehensible, decent, flammable, opportune, sufficient

| Test Seven | COMMON CITIES | Question 4 |

What have the following towns or cities in common?

Bath, Bury, Cork, Reading, Slough, Wells, York

| Test Seven | ODD ONE OUT | Question 5 |

Which is the odd one out from:

second, minute, hour, day, week, fortnight, month

| Test Seven | IDENTICAL MONTHS | Question 6 |

Which calendar months are identical in a non-leap year? What about in a leap year?

Using a standard keyboard can you use only adjacent letters to make a nine-letter word?

What property is shared by the letters 'F' and 'J' and no others?

Why can the following groups of three letters be considered to be in alphabetical order?

bnn, ule, oyx, oer, btl, luy, ile

Following on from 609... why are these in order?

jet, bke, ugl, aen, fiy, lit, otc, ack

Which is the odd name out?

Dennis, Delia, Edward, Liam, Tessa

What is the link between these pairs of names?

Trotsky & Gallagher; Marx & Winfrey; Pauling & Gavaskar

| Test Seven | WHAT ARE THEY? | Question 13 |

What are the following?

Charcot, Romeo, Altair, Faradya, Josephine

| Test Seven | INTERPRETATION | Question 14 |

How may the following be interpreted?

timing, tim ing

| Test Seven | MUSICAL ABBREVIATION | Question 15 |

The two letters mp represent a musical abbreviation. What does it have in common with anagrams?

| Test Seven | MISSING AMOUNT | Question 16 |

What is missing from the following:

fluid ounce, gill, pint, quart, ????, peck, bushel, quarter?

| Test Seven | YEAR LINKS | Question 17 |

What links the years 1066, 1483 and 1936?

| Test Seven | IN COMMON | Question 18 |

What do the following have in common?

Charing Cross Station, Paris, Hammersmith, Laredo, Venus, Mayfair, Tintagel, The Strand

| Test Seven | NINE MEANINGS | Question 19 |

Can you find two three-letter words which differ only by their initial letter? They are pronounced differently and between them have at least nine meanings.

| Test Seven | MOBILE PLACES | Question 20 |

Where can you find Glasgow in Cornwall, Windsor Castle in Middlesex and Chepstow in Surrey?

| Test Seven | EMPTY | Question 21 |

Which two Japanese words, both meaning 'empty-something' have been assimilated into English?

| Test Seven | ANALGESIC | Question 22 |

How does adding a letter to a common analgesic produce 'aiming for recognition'?

| Test Seven | ALPHABETICAL? | Question 23 |

How could these words be said to be in alphabetical order?

aviary, seedy, decay, arty, escapee, excellency

---

**DID YOU KNOW?**
A million million nerve cells are packed into every human head. There are as many cells between your ears as there are stars in the Milky Way galaxy.

Arrange these six words into pairs to form three new words. How long does each last?

IN
CHI
RUM
LUST
LEAD
DICTION

Which two letters complete the following?

Brains, Fancy, Benny, Cho Cho

A hunter chases a bear for three miles due north and then due south for a further two miles. What is the maximum distance he can be from where he began the hunt?

What have the following in common?

bras, cosines, cares, princes

Which, numerically, is the odd one out?

fretwork, freighter, frigate, frightened

**LONG MEDICAL WORD**

What 17-letter medical word contains three double letters (M, P, S), and four other letters (I, N, O, U) which each appear twice?

**THAT IS THE QUESTION**

to a question put to a famous composer was '9W'. What might have been the question? The Test Seven nswer

**NUMBER SERIES**

Which number follows in this series?

3, 3, 5, 4, 4, 3, 6, 5, 4, 3

**DOUBLE LETTERS**

Find a word containing two double 'B's and one with two double 'P's

**ODD ONE OUT**

Which is the odd one out?

won, who, we, wore, hive, wicks, what, wait, whine, when

**FIVE EEZY PIECES**

What nine-letter word has five 'E's in it

| Test Seven | ONE MILLION | Question 35 |
| --- | --- | --- |

Which two numbers that do not contain any zeros, produce exactly 1,000,000, when multiplied together?

| Test Seven | THREE-LETTER PARTS | Question 36 |
| --- | --- | --- |

Can you name ten familiar parts of the human body, each of which comprises only three letters?

| Test Seven | WORD GAMES | Question 37 |
| --- | --- | --- |

Continue the following sequence:

1, 3, 3, 2, 1, 4, 2, 4, 1, 8, ??

(Clue: Think of word games.)

| Test Seven | NAME CONNECTION | Question 38 |
| --- | --- | --- |

What is the connection between the following names?

Gamaliel, Swinomish, Rudolph

| Test Seven | LETTERING AND COLOURING | Question 39 |
| --- | --- | --- |

What is coloured red if it is lettered 'A', cream if lettered 'A/B', blue if lettered 'A/B/C' and black if lettered 'B/C'?

| Test Seven | SYMBOLS? | Question 40 |

On what type of document would you find the following symbols and what do they mean?

A circle with a dot at the centre and a triangle with a dot at the centre.

| Test Seven | COMMON FEATURE | Question 41 |

What do the following words have in common?

cease, wheat, cat, set, sank, cans, meal, says

| Test Seven | PAPER TABLE | Question 42 |

When is a table like a newspaper?

| Test Seven | AUSTRALIAN PLACE NAME | Question 43 |

Which place name in Australia contains 13 letters, eight of them the same?

| Test Seven | ENGLISH PLACE NAME | Question 44 |

Which place name in England contains 14 letters, none of them the same?

| Test Seven | HISTORICAL CHARACTERS | Question 45 |

What do the following ten historical characters have in common?

Daedalus, Hannibal, Octavius, Prince Leopold, Gustavus, Moses, Attila, Caractacus, Cicero and Galileo

| Test Seven | **SECOND LETTER CHANGE** | Question 46 |
|---|---|---|

Two European countries differ in spelling only because the second letter in their names is different. What are they?

| Test Seven | **SERIES** | Question 47 |
|---|---|---|

Jason, DJ, FM/AM, ?? What completes the series?

| Test Seven | **US CONNECTION** | Question 48 |
|---|---|---|

Which of these is the odd one out? (Clue: There is a US connection.)

Raleigh, Cromwell, Lincoln, Bismarck, Montgomery

| Test Seven | **ANIMAL MINISTERS** | Question 49 |
|---|---|---|

Can you think of two British prime ministers such that when you remove the first letter of their names, animal abodes are revealed?

| Test Seven | **BRITISH CONFLICTS** | Question 50 |
|---|---|---|

In the twentieth century, British troops have fought in conflicts involving the Orange Free State, Germany, Brunei, Northern Ireland, Argentina and Iraq.

What is unusual about this list?

| Test Seven | **SYLLABLES** | Question 51 |
|---|---|---|

Which 15-letter word is usually pronounced in two syllables?

Which 5-letter word is usually pronounced in four syllables?

| Test Seven | SPORTS FIGURES | Question 52 |

Can you think of three geometric figures which are also playing arenas for different sports?

| Test Seven | PHONETICS | Question 53 |

The name of which car company is very similar to two words used in the International Phonetic Alphabet?

| Test Seven | ODD ONES OUT | Question 54 |

Which two of the following are odd ones out?

Christ Church, Corpus Christi, Jesus, King's, Pembroke, St Catherine's, St John's, Trinity, Wolfson

| Test Seven | CHRONOLOGICAL | Question 55 |

What is the connection in the following chronologically based sequence?

hypermarket, green, Watergate, F-word, punk, detox, Trekkie, naff all, trainers, karaoke

| Test Seven | BIRD REPRESENTATION | Question 56 |

Which bird is represented by the following?

Par
2

| Test Seven | TRANSPOSED YEARS | Question 57 |

If nine is added to my age its two digits are transposed. This has been the case in six other years of my life. How old am I?

| Test Seven | UNUSUAL SHAPES | Question 58 |

Where might you find a group of objects shaped like a boat, a moon, a pea, a hook and a head?

| Test Seven | ODD ONE OUT | Question 59 |

Which of the following is the odd one out and why?

Nick Faldo, Eric Idle, Elton John, Josef Stalin, Tim Rice, Adolf Hitler, Nick Nolte

| Test Seven | EIGHT CONSONANTS | Question 60 |

Which country's name begins with eight consonants when spelt in English?

| Test Seven | COMMON FEATURE | Question 61 |

What do the following have in common?

burn, dream, lean, learn, spoil

| Test Seven | DANCING | Question 62 |

How does adding an English indefinite article to a Greek letter produce a Latin American dance?

| Test Seven | ODD ONE OUT | Question 63 |

Which of the following is the odd one out?

acute, cedilla, circumflex, diaeresis, grave, tilda, umlaut

What is the connection between the number 10, a 10p coin and the lower value coins, i.e. 1p, 2p and 5p?

What is never odd or even?

(Clue: lateral thinking is required.)

What is the connection between footballer Leon Noel and the designer of the Eden Project in Cornwall?

What is the link between the following words?

agape, bow, desert (noun), lead, putting, sow, wind, wound

Complete the following sentence with two different seven-letter words. The words used must be anagrams, i.e. the same seven letters must be used for both words.

He has been her ? on ? occasions.

What do the following have in common?

bg, dn, pp, pt, tn

How many minutes is it before 12 noon if 57 minutes ago it was twice as many minutes past 9am?

What do the following pairs of countries have in common?

Algeria + Sudan; Mali + Qatar; Belarus + India; Italy + Gabon

What do these words have in common:

aye, can, do, go, paw, tar, tom

If the latest two of a long-running film series are TWINE and DAD, what was the first?

Why might Eliza Doolittle have had difficulty naming the four stars of the film *My Fair Lady*?

What word can be placed in front of all the words below to produce, in each case, a familiar word or phrase?

entry, standard, check, space

Can you think of a 13-letter word which features the same vowel four times and has only three other consonants?

Many English words change from masculine to feminine when a suffix is added. Which is the only one to change from feminine to masculine?

You have ten columns, each containing ten coins of identical appearance. All of the coins weigh 1 ounce except those in one of the columns, which weigh 2 ounces each.

With a set of scales (not balance), identify the rogue column with only one weighing.

If (Venus + Earth) × Neptune = 40 how much is (Jupiter − Mercury) × Pluto?

Athlete 4 always beats Athlete 1, while Athlete 2 beats 3, but loses to 1. Who finishes last?

Can you name three units of measurement which sound like three consecutive letters of the alphabet?

Which element concludes this sequence?

Aluminium, Boron, Erbium, Tellurium, Indium, Sulphur, Tellurium, ???

Which of the following is the odd one out?

Chico, Harpo, Zeppo, Karlo and Groucho

Organise the following into pairs:

Einstein, Nelson, Herschel, Talbot, Caesar

Uranus, Rome, e = mc squared, Aboukir, Castillon

Where will you find canaries, eagles, foxes, owls and wolves in (relative) harmony?

What eleven-letter word uses only one vowel but uses it five times?

What thirteen-letter word uses only one vowel but uses it five times?

Which is the odd one out? (Clue: think of a foreign language.)

main, loin, wain, coin, pain

Can you think of a place name which is in an English-speaking country (but not in the UK) which has twelve letters including one which is used eight times?

Which of these words is the odd one out?

any, buy, do, eye, for, of, one, two, who

Find a word of five letters. The clue is paper. Each successive letter begins an anagram of the word. The four clues for the new words are: things, small creatures, gives out, strike.

What do the following words have in common?

aisle, gauge, knave, plumb, scent, write

Stephen is one and a half times as old as Nigel, who is one and a half times as old as Dennis. Their ages total 152 years. How old is Nigel?

Mary has four times as many as Sally and Sally has three times as many as Tony. Altogether they have 64. How many has Sally?

What do the following words have in common?

Deer, Dress, Look, Poll, Sew, Tresses, Was

Fred and Joe both have £1,000. Fred bets Joe £100 that if Joe gives Fred £200 Fred will give him £300 back. If the transaction proceeds, who will benefit?

When was the last year in which someone could have been born in order to live in a year which was the square of their age?

Pungent is to taste as ......... is to sound.

Is it muted, cacophonous, muffled or deafening?

It is possible to add a single letter (not the same one) to the following words to create a group of items which go together. There is one exception. What is the group and which is the rogue word?

able, hair, ivan, lock, ouch, rock, tool

The name of the spoken and written language of which state is a palindrome?

---

**DID YOU KNOW?**

Practitioners of mind sports are fascinated by the relative difficulty of their different pastimes. The approximate number of possible positions available in the most popular mind sports is as follows.

Shogi is the Japanese version of chess, in which captured pieces defect to the opposite side, while XiangQi is the type of chess played in China, where pieces include the elephant and a central river divides the board in two.

| | |
|---|---|
| Go | $10^{170}$ |
| Scrabble | $10^{150}$ |
| Poker | $10^{72}$ |
| Shogi | $10^{70}$ |
| Chess | $10^{50}$ |
| XiangQi | $10^{50}$ |
| Bridge | $10^{30}$ |
| Draughts | $10^{20}$ |
| Backgammon | $10^{19}$ |

---

# TEST EIGHT

| Test Eight | DIGITAL CLOCK | Question 1 |
|---|---|---|

I have a digital clock which does not show zero before a single digit hour. How often during a 24 hour period will the sections forming the figures on the minute side of the clock be the exact mirror image of those on the hour side, with the dots dead centre?

| Test Eight | DIGITAL CLOCK SEQUENCE | Question 2 |
|---|---|---|

Continuing the digital clock theme, what does the following sequence represent?

6 2 5 5 4 5 6 3 7 6

| Test Eight | ODD ONE OUT | Question 3 |
|---|---|---|

Which is the odd-one-out here?

English, hyphenated, mellifluous, noun, polysyllabic, short, sibilant, word

| Test Eight | BIBLICAL PLURAL | Question 4 |
|---|---|---|

There is a Biblical word which, when you add an 's' at the end, changes from plural to singular, and when you add an additional 'es' becomes plural again, but only half as many as originally. What is the word?

| Test Eight | CONNECTION | Question 5 |
|---|---|---|

Can you find a connection between anagrams of the following six words?

Handy butchers near Harlem large whingers

Can you arrange six digits 0 to 5 in a triangle so that the sum of the 3 digits along each side is the same?

What do the following have in common?

Arthur Turner, Rev. Mr Wilks, Cellini, The Crawley Beauty, Tom Putt

How can you arrange the numbers 1 to 8 at the corners of a cube so that the sum of the numbers on each face is the same?

If George is 1, Abraham is 5 and Ulysses 50, then who is 100 and what are they?

What infamous distinction attaches to Popes Celestine V, Nicholas III and Archbishop Ruggieri?

On a bird watching expedition one member claims to have seen a nye, another a fall, a third a walk, and the final one a sege

What have they been looking at?

| Test Eight | TWO, TWO AND THREE | Question 12 |
|---|---|---|

The Duke of Wellington is 2, Disraeli is also 2, but Edward Stanley is 3. What do the numbers represent?

| Test Eight | CUBITT, OMER AND EPHAN | Question 13 |
|---|---|---|

Where are cubitt, omer and ephan to be found?

| Test Eight | LITERARY LINK | Question 14 |
|---|---|---|

What links Marlowe, Goethe, Thomas Mann, Boito Gounod and Delacroix?

| Test Eight | FEEL THE FEAR | Question 15 |
|---|---|---|

What should a person suffering from spheksophobia, arachnophobia and selachophobia avoid?

| Test Eight | TITLES | Question 16 |
|---|---|---|

Where might one use the following titles?

grand inspector inquisitor commander
sublime prince of the royal secret
sovereign grand inspector general

| Test Eight | SIXTEEN DOTS | Question 17 |
|---|---|---|

Imagine 16 dots laid out in the form of a 4 × 4 square. These are numbered 1–4 in the first row, 5–8 in the second etc. Place a pencil at any point and then using only straight lines and without lifting your pencil from the paper connect all the dots. What is the minimum number of straight lines required to do this?

| Test Eight | COLLECTORS | Question 18 |

Match the following collections with collectors:

arctophile, bibliophile, tegestologist, incunabilist, philatelist

stamps, teddy bears, early books, books in general, beer mats

| Test Eight | TREE | Question 19 |

In what tree would you find a tall chair, a big gate, a wide field, a huge purse, and lots of little men?

| Test Eight | PAIR OF ACES | Question 20 |

If you play a pair of aces after a deuce, what do you win?

| Test Eight | SEVEN-LETTER WORDS | Question 21 |

Can you think of five seven-letter words that are the same except for a single vowel change?

---

**DID YOU KNOW?**
Throughout a pregnancy, the baby's brain is growing extremely quickly. In fact at one stage of prenatal brain development the brain is producing roughly a quarter of a million new neurons every single minute. This is a staggering amount and it is one of the reasons why pregnant women get so tired.

What links the following words?

close, devil, height, mover, trough, your

What is the connection between the following?

land snail – 4, 1; human – 0, 2; starfish – 0, 5; ant – 2, 6; spider – 0, 8;
horseshoe crab – 0, 10; butterfly – 2, 10

Which Cambridgeshire hospital, famous for heart transplant surgery, sounds as though it is of little value?

Gus is to Virgil as Buzz is to Edwin; in what context?

Two owner jockeys bet each other that their own horse is slower than the other's over six furlongs (not their usual distance). What is the quickest way to resolve the issue?

What completes the following list?

hexagon – none
pentagon – dodecahedron
square – cube
triangle – icosahedron
octahedron – ??

A boat is moored at a dock that has a ladder with rungs 9 inches apart, 12 visible above the waterline. The boat has a ladder over its side, with rungs 6 inches apart, showing 10 above the waterline. The tide is rising at 1 foot per hour. How many rungs will be visible on each ladder after three hours?

What three nine-letter words contain the five vowels once only and are anagrams of each other?

Can you find at least eight different ways of spelling the phonetic sound nu (as in nude)?

Which of the following is the odd one out?

pas de deux, plie, entrechat, touche

Where in London must you drive on the right hand side of the road?

If Cantuar, Ebor, Petriburg and Roffen were to meet – what exactly would you have?

With which activity are the following words associated?

eyer, stoop, inke, jenk

What do the following words have in common?

colour, defence, draught, litre, metre, gramme, plough

Can you think of two words that do not rhyme and yet end in the same eight letters?

What is the connection between a big garment, a type of spreadsheet, and the number 40?

| Test Eight | UNUSUAL ARITHMETIC | Question 38 |

What form of arithmetic is being used in the following?

2 + 10 = 20; 2 × 10 = 17; 17 – 2 = 11; 17 ÷ 2 = 2; 2 + 2 = 11

| Test Eight | STRANGE OBJECT | Question 39 |

What has a head but no feet, branches but no roots, and a bank but no money?

| Test Eight | STRANGE CREATURE | Question 40 |

What has one head, four legs and one foot?

| Test Eight | FOUR WORDS | Question 41 |

Find four words which mean the following and are uniquely related in some way.

a trap                                          anything in Yorkshire
Greek letters                                ex-member of Roxy music

| Test Eight | FOREIGN EXPRESSION | Question 42 |

Find a familiar foreign expression of just eight letters (two words) which contains all five vowels.

| Test Eight | AIR TRAVEL | Question 43 |

Which two international air transport companies are each represented by certain contiguous sections of the alphabet?

| Test Eight | GROOVY | Question 44 |

A standard vinyl single record rotates at 45 rpm, and has sides A and B, each of which runs for 2.5 min. In total, how many grooves does it have?

| Test Eight | COMMON WORDS | Question 45 |

What do the following have in common?

Angstrom, blessed, debut, expose, lame, naive, resume, role, Zaire

| Test Eight | SAME PHENOMENON | Question 46 |

Rather than being considered as opposites, in which field have the terms WIMP and MACHO been postulated to explain the same phenomenon?

| Test Eight | FOUR SPORTS | Question 47 |

Which four common sports use, what approximate to, prolate spheroids?

| Test Eight | BIOLOGICAL | Question 48 |

A is to T as C is to G; in what (biological) context?

| Test Eight | UNUSUAL ALPHABET | Question 49 |

How may the following be put into alphabetical order without changing the sequence of words?

frame, notice, word, string, ring, bend, shirt, turn, sign, ray, fronts

Cropping the corners off the English St George's Cross flag cannot produce the Irish St Patrick's flag (even though they are both red crosses on a white background). Why not?

Austria and Denmark are contiguous neighbours of the UK. How?

What is the connection between the following?

cembalo scrivano, chirographer, clavier imprimeur, mechanical typographer, rapigraphe, universal compositor

Which famous novel has the same three letters, in the same order, at the beginning and end of its title?

What is unique about the numbers 1, 6, 7 and 4 in the context of the possible 4-digit numbers they can make?

What is the connection between the capital city of Lebanon, and the Bavarian city most associated with Richard Wagner?

If 'whale' is to 'shark' as 'zebra' is to 'fish', then 'stag' is to ... what?

How does the following list relate to 1967?

1 None; 2 Light; 3 Third; 4 Home

Which animal provides the link between: John Updike, Richard Adams and Chas and Dave?

What English word consists of five letter 'E's with two consonants between each pair of 'E'?

Add a different letter, in the same position, to each of the following (there is a logical progression), to produce a new word. The new word alters the pronunciation of the existing one.

lower, earth, slander, aunt, eyed, over, allow, ether, dour, lease

Continue the sequence: E, O, E, R, E, .........

Arrange the following in order of speed:

blackbird, bluebird, mallard, robin

Which of the following is the odd one out?

bactrian, camelopard, dromedary, guanaco, llama, vicuña

In what sense does having a hip replacement equate to a Greek letter?

What is the significance of the following equation?

$5(F - 32) = 9C$

What is the reasoning behind the division of the following London railway termini into two groups?

Fenchurch St, King's Cross, Liverpool St, Marylebone
Charing Cross, Euston, Paddington, Victoria, Waterloo

| Test Eight | COMMON WORDS | Question 67 |
|---|---|---|

What do the following have in common?

art, crossover, hard, pomp, progressive, psychedelic, space, stadium

| Test Eight | ODD ONE OUT | Question 68 |
|---|---|---|

Which of the following is the odd one out?

boson, electron, fermion, neutron, nucleon, pluton, proton

| Test Eight | AGEING | Question 69 |
|---|---|---|

I am four times as old as my brother and in two years time I will be just three times as old. In how many years will I be twice as old as my brother?

| Test Eight | NOT ANATOMY | Question 70 |
|---|---|---|

Rather than anatomy, what is the connection between GUT, TOE and 42?

---

**DID YOU KNOW?**
In 1984 the political scientist James Flynn reported that Americans had gained about 13.8 IQ points in 46 years. If people taking an IQ test today were scored in the same way as people 50 years ago then 90% of them would be classified in the genius level.

Which of the following words is the odd one out?

elision, hyperbole, irony, litotes, metaphor, oxymoron, paradox

Which type of tree is missing (marked *) from the following representation of a British town?

LYNE
*TON

What is the distinction between the items in the following lists?

abductor, Achilles, extensor, flexor, hamstring
cruciate, medial collateral, peridontal, suspensory

Which household object, often abbreviated to two letters, is formed from a mix of Greek and Latin roots?

### DID YOU KNOW?

Your brain uses less power than your refrigerator light. The brain uses 12 watts of power. Over the course of a day, your brain uses the amount of energy contained in two large bananas. Curiously, even though the brain is very efficient, it's an energy hog. It is only 3% of the body's weight, but consumes 17% of the body's total energy. Most of its energy costs go into maintenance; the added cost of thinking hard is barely noticeable..

What is the connection in the following list?

Jimmy Durante – Nose
Claudia Schiffer – Face
Dolly Parton – Breasts
Liberace, Richard Clayderman, Keith Richards – Hands
Cyd Charisse, Fred Astaire, Betty Grable – Legs

Which three types of human muscle are given names derived from geometric forms: one triangle and two quadrilaterals?

What is the connection in the following list?

1 Algeria, Greece, Turkey
2 Belgium, Brazil
3 Australia, Denmark
4 Indonesia, Senegal

When viewing a standard 12-hour digital clock display the number 23 is of interest as it represents two possible maximums. What are these maximums?

What is the African connection for the following people: actors Michael Gambon and Art Malik; MPs Tony Benn and David Cameron?

| Test Eight | CRAZY CAR | Question 80 |

What car can go backwards as well as forwards?

| Test Eight | SIX CREATURES | Question 81 |

Make six creatures out of the following:

shark, dog, monkey, elephant, kangaroo, spider, fly, whale, shrew, fish, rat, horse

| Test Eight | TWO YEAR DIFFERENCE | Question 82 |

Can you use all ten digits to write down two years and the difference between them?

| Test Eight | SEQUENCE | Question 83 |

What follows in this sequence:

st, nd, rd, th, ...?

| Test Eight | SPORTING POSITION | Question 84 |

Which sporting position does 'flah' represent?

| Test Eight | THREE GROUPS | Question 85 |

What is the reasoning behind the division of the following into three groups?

comma, full-stop;
colon, exclamation mark, question mark, semi-colon;
ellipsis

| Test Eight | SEA FLOORS | Question 86 |

Which English town, together with its county, could describe some sea floors?

| Test Eight | ODD ONE OUT | Question 87 |

Which of the following is the odd one out?

complex, imaginary, irrational, natural, rational, real, synthetic, transcendental, transfinite

| Test Eight | PERIODIC TABLE | Question 88 |

In the Periodic Table, how are elements 92, 93, 94 linked with the Solar System?

| Test Eight | HOMOPHONES | Question 89 |

Which two homophones may be used in conjunction with sugar and/or oil?

| Test Eight | PLACES | Question 90 |

What is the connection in the following list?

Buenos Aires, Tirana, Vienna (1,1); Sofia (2,1); Ottawa (3,1); London (5,4); Paris (6,5)

| Test Eight | INTERNET EXCELLENCE | Question 91 |

How can internet excellence produce the same status?

If chemist = 9032 and chess = 9033 why does factions = 9034?

Which famous composer has a three character string from the word 'October' in both his first name and surname?

Which area of France may be represented by the following list?

A B C D E F G H I J K L N O P Q S T U V W X Z

Which two homophones may be used in geometry, music and anatomy?

In cricket, if each batsman is clean bowled by successive balls from the first one bowled (i.e. the first ten balls, in six-ball overs), which number batsman remains not out?

Which word connects the delimiting line between the sunlit and shadowed sides of the Moon, and Arnold Schwarzenegger?

What do the following have in common?

addition, cracking, elimination, precipitation, reduction, substitution, synthesis

Of which organ is a meninx (singular noun) a surrounding membrane, inflammation (derived from the plural) of which could be fatal?

What completes the following sequence:

exclamation, double quotes, pound, dollar, percentage, .........

# TEST NINE

| Test Nine | MATHEMATICAL TERM | Question 1 |
|---|---|---|

Which mathematical term provides the link between Sir Isaac Newton, Gottfried Leibniz, and George Remi (Hergé)?

| Test Nine | TIE-BREAK | Question 2 |
|---|---|---|

In a tie-break in a Wimbledon doubles, player A serves the first point from the Royal Box end. If all points are won by the server, what is the score when she next has to serve from that end?

| Test Nine | SHARED FEATURE | Question 3 |
|---|---|---|

What feature is shared by the following three four-letter words?

mite, star, spot

| Test Nine | NUMBER TWO | Question 4 |
|---|---|---|

An acronym for the number 2 could be O.P.E.N.

Can you explain this? (Clue: the number 2 has a unique property.)

| Test Nine | ALPHABETICAL NUMBER | Question 5 |
|---|---|---|

Can you find a number that can be written using letters in alphabetical order?

| Test Nine | SCORERS | Question 6 |
|---|---|---|

If Wayne Rooney scores one, and Clint Eastwood scores 2, how many does David Attenborough score?

| Test Nine | COMMON WORDS | Question 7 |

What do the following words have in common?

number, shirt, day, ray, bend, turn

| Test Nine | REVERSE ALPHABETICAL NUMBERS | Question 8 |

How many numbers have their letters written in reverse alphabetical order?

| Test Nine | ODD ONE OUT | Question 9 |

Which is the odd one out in this list?

stop, emit, trap, clip, teem, tips, tuba, spin, tram

| Test Nine | UNIQUE MONTHS | Question 10 |

What property is shared by March, May and August and by no other months?

| Test Nine | COUNTRY LINK | Question 11 |

What is the link between:

Bolivia and Guinea
Austria and Peru
Hungary and Italy

| Test Nine | BRITNEY | Question 12 |

After rehabilitation, to which religious group might Britney Spears resort?

The following is part of a commonly encountered series of digits: 10111212. What immediately precedes it?

Which capital city is written using an ellipsis (a row of three dots ...)?

How can the following words be turned into five of a kind: royal, red, cardinal, giant, brave?

How does inserting one particular time-period into another, complementary one, produce a sequence of international significance?

In what sport are two winged beasts used to avoid another winged beast?

Which two European nationalities are still employed in the restoration of antique furniture?

Jane is four times as old as James, but in six years time she will only be twice as old. How old are Jane and James now?

What orthographical ability do the following words share?

bag, last, mass, mate, pack, patting

Can you name the big band leader with all the vowels?

Which two composers might help you to remember what you need at the supermarket?

Which five mutual anagrams describe another composer's frosty response to an offer of alcohol?

Can you think of a familiar sequence which increases as follows?

the second is twice the first
the third is two and a half times the second
the fourth is twice the third
the fifth is twice the fourth
the sixth is two and a half times the fifth
the seventh is twice the sixth

| Test Nine | DOMINO ON A CHESSBOARD | Question 25 |
| --- | --- | --- |

Imagine a normal 8 × 8 chessboard with the a1 and h8 squares removed (bottom left and top right). A domino covers precisely two squares. Can you cover this board with dominos and leave no gaps?

| Test Nine | WHERE ARE THEY? | Question 26 |
| --- | --- | --- |

Where would you have expected to find the following:

andabata, myrmillo, secutor, retiarius?

| Test Nine | NOBLE, BEAUTIFUL, ??? | Question 27 |
| --- | --- | --- |

If horse racing is the sport of kings, boxing is the noble art and the beautiful game is football, what is the tesserarian art?

| Test Nine | ODD ONE OUT | Question 28 |
| --- | --- | --- |

Which is the odd one out?

ant, spider, fly, beetle, ladybird, cockroach

| Test Nine | OPPOSITES | Question 29 |
| --- | --- | --- |

Why are stakhanovism and oblomovism opposites?

| Test Nine | ODD ONE OUT | Question 30 |
| --- | --- | --- |

Which is the odd one out?

Austerlitz, Marengo, Jena, Blenheim, Wagram

Which Roman connection is the odd one out?

Zephyrinus, Incitatus, Eleutherius, Anacletus, Telesphorus

If a two sports competition is a biathlon what respectively are three, four, five, seven and ten?

Assuming you have two standard six-sided dice how many ways are there of throwing a total of 10, 7 and 3?

What is unusual about the months January and October (this changes to January and July during a leap year)?

What is the link between the following places:

Southampton, Northampton, St Helens, New Orleans, St Kilda?

Which of the following is the odd one out?

pangolin, pismire, aardvark, echidna

| Test Nine | I'M A BELIEVER | Question 37 |
|---|---|---|

What would you be if you believed in any of the following?

donatism, pelagianism, nestorianism, monophysitisum, monothelitism

| Test Nine | UNITED | Question 38 |
|---|---|---|

What unites Malta, Tamburlaine, Edward II and Dr Faustus?

| Test Nine | DODECAHEDRON | Question 39 |
|---|---|---|

How many faces does a regular dodecahedron have and what shape are they?

| Test Nine | DANGEROUS PLACE | Question 40 |
|---|---|---|

Many millions of people are admitted to UK hospitals each year. Try arranging the following causes in order of most common starting with most and ending with least.

a) contact with hornets
b) falling off a chair
c) alligator bite
d) pyjamas set on fire

| Test Nine | BAD IDEA | Question 41 |
|---|---|---|

Why are polyandry, adelphogamy and pantagamy generally frowned on in the UK?

| Test Nine | COMMON WORDS | Question 42 |
|---|---|---|

What do wolf, hay, harvest and hunters have in common?

| Test Nine | COMMON COMPLAINTS | Question 43 |

Why are epidermophyton floccosum, plantar fasciitis and abductor tendinitis directly opposite to central palmar blister and distal ulnar neuropathy?

| Test Nine | BRISK | Question 44 |

How does adding a letter to a synonym of 'briskly' produce a Native American?

| Test Nine | NOT IN THE USA | Question 45 |

Which cardinal point of the compass is not represented by a state of the USA?

| Test Nine | NOVEL CONNECTION | Question 46 |

What is the connection between the following series of novels: Perry Mason cases, Emma Harte saga (including A Woman of Substance), Leatherstocking Tales (including The Last of the Mohicans)?

| Test Nine | PUNCTUATION | Question 47 |

Which of the following is the odd one out?

backslash, oblique dash, slash, stroke, solidus, virgule

| Test Nine | LINK | Question 48 |

Which name provides the link between: erstwhile pop duo Sonny and Cher; Paul Hewson of pop group U2; the original proponent of lateral thinking?

Which is the odd one out?

belisarius, helianthus, marcellus, germanicus, fabius, crassus, pompeius

What new items may be made by adding precious substances to the following?

birch, blonde, finch, isle, rattlesnake

The following are anagrams of names of languages: REES, AMARGY. To which countries do they belong?

What do the following have in common?

buy, pair, praise, rain, road, sew, to, vain

What is the distinction between the items in following lists?

mean, median, mode

bell-shape, skew, standard deviation, variance

| Test Nine | EUROPEAN FOOD | Question 54 |

Which two types of European food are anagrams of a five-letter phrase meaning 'an earlier time'?

| Test Nine | CHINESE FOOD | Question 55 |

Which type of Chinese food is the reverse of a six-letter phrase meaning 'a later time'?

| Test Nine | ODD PLACE OUT | Question 56 |

Which is the odd one in the following sequence:

Equatorial Guinea, Gabon, Congo, Democratic Republic of Congo, Uganda, Kenya, Somalia?

| Test Nine | PALINDROMIC HERO | Question 57 |

The name of which Greek hero contains three palindromes?

| Test Nine | LINKING WORD | Question 58 |

What word links Custer, Mohicans and Fermat?

| Test Nine | COUNTRYSIDE | Question 59 |

Which part of the British countryside can be attained in judo and karate?

| Test Nine | HEAVY BRICK | Question 60 |

If a brick weighs 3 kilos plus the weight of half a brick what does a brick and a half weigh?

How does inserting a type of radiation into a blunder produce the tallest living animal?

Which is the odd one out?

cretaceous, sebaceous, carboniferous, miocene, pliocene, pleistocene

Why should the symbol for a racehorse be a goat?

What is the connection between the following:

England, Mexico, South Wales, Hampshire, York

Who should be careful not to harm any frogs when putting on shoes?

How does inserting a pronoun, which sounds like one sensory organ, into a second, produce something that could be detected by a third sensory organ?

| Test Nine | GOL | Question 67 |
|---|---|---|

How does 'gol' equate to arrears of uncompleted work?

| Test Nine | PHILOSOPHICAL WELL | Question 68 |
|---|---|---|

How does adding a capital letter to a type of well produce a word relating to René Descartes?

| Test Nine | ODD ONE OUT | Question 69 |
|---|---|---|

Which of the following is the odd one out?

clock, magnetic compass, plumb line, protractor, slide rule, sextant, vernier callipers

| Test Nine | LEPORIDAE | Question 70 |
|---|---|---|

Which US eastern seaboard resort and amusement park was named after its Leporidae population?

| Test Nine | SERIES | Question 71 |
|---|---|---|

What completes the following series:

egg, larva, pupa, ...

| Test Nine | NEARLY DONE | Question 72 |
|---|---|---|

In what way can both 'ked' and 'coc' be interpreted in terms of being only partly ready?

| Test Nine | CRICKET MATCH | Question 73 |

Why would you need these for a cricket match?

a hat, a spare blanket, a book (by Graham Greene)

| Test Nine | ALL OF THEM | Question 74 |

Which word is all of these?

transgression; Hebrew letter; trigonometric abbreviation

| Test Nine | FREAKY EXPERIMENT | Question 75 |

Which word links the following?

experiment; freak; a key used to change the functionality of another key on a computer keyboard

| Test Nine | ADDING | Question 76 |

What can you add to the following?

black, clip, cup, floor, over, skate, spring, star, surf

| Test Nine | ODD ONE OUT | Question 77 |

Which of the following is the odd one out?

adroit, chiral, dextrous, gauche, limbic, sinister

| Test Nine | CHRISTMAS GIFTS | Question 78 |

By the twelfth day of Christmas, I shall have received 12 partridges, 22 turtle doves etc. Which present(s) is (are) the most numerous?

| Test Nine | TOTAL PRESENTS | Question 79 |

What is the total number of presents received?

| Test Nine | ODD ONE OUT | Question 80 |

Which is the odd one out?

golf, Quebec, hotel, beach, India, whisky

| Test Nine | WHO'S NOT WELCOME? | Question 81 |

Which is the odd one out?

Newton, Pascal, Hertz, Descartes, Kelvin, Watt

| Test Nine | NUMBER SIX | Question 82 |

Why does the number 6 get bigger the more you take away?

(Clue: consider different ways of representing numbers.)

| Test Nine | TERMINAL | Question 83 |

What was terminal about the following dates?

44BC, 1793, 1865, 1914, 1948, 1980

| Test Nine | PLACES | Question 84 |
|---|---|---|

If Iran is to Persia as Turkey is to Asia Minor, then Thailand is to ... where?

| Test Nine | PRESIDENTIAL CONNECTION | Question 85 |
|---|---|---|

What links Bart Simpson's friend Milhouse, Bart's grandmother and Kermit the Frog with Presidents Nixon, Kennedy and Roosevelt?

| Test Nine | ALABAMA | Question 86 |
|---|---|---|

Which city and port of Alabama, USA, looks as if it is not fixed in place?

| Test Nine | COMMON PLACES | Question 87 |
|---|---|---|

What do the following places have in common?

Arlen, Texas; Bedrock; Jellystone Park; Langley Falls; Manhattan; Quahog; Springfield

| Test Nine | HIGH WOOD | Question 88 |
|---|---|---|

Which instrument derives its name from high wood?

| Test Nine | THREE HERBS | Question 89 |
|---|---|---|

Which line of a song by Otis Redding mentions three herbs?

| Test Nine | SURVIVORS | Question 90 |
|---|---|---|

The surviving members of which group are called James and Richard?

If fiction is to science as lit is to chick, then ripper is to … what?

In its most common form, which game has as its aim to score in one of 82 areas?

As which part of Kenya may the following be interpreted?

L Y
A E
V L

What is the connection between the following animals?

antelope, cattle, elephant, elk, giraffe, whale

Which North American province, called Acadia when occupied by the French, now has a name derived from Latin?

What have the following people in common?

Jean de Dinteville, Georges de Selve, Susan Tilley, Jonathan Buttall

Which tree fruit is an anagram of the type of tree on which it grows?

A clock takes exactly two seconds to strike two o'clock. How long will it take to strike three o'clock?

What do all these words have in common?

gem, yak, map, dine, lien, mail, nave, ailed, asset, nomad

Which of the following transits across the face of the Sun, as viewed from the Earth, is the odd one out?

asteroid, comet, Mars, Mercury, Moon, Venus

# TEST TEN

| Test Ten | GENRES | Question 1 |
|---|---|---|

What is the difference between the two lists of genres?

1. romantic comedy, science fiction, situation comedy
2. costume drama, creature feature, swords and sandals

| Test Ten | POSH TERM | Question 2 |
|---|---|---|

If I said 'thermospa' was a posh term for a hot tub, why would I be using mixed metaphors?

| Test Ten | PREFIX | Question 3 |
|---|---|---|

How does prefixing the first word in each pair with a pronoun, produce the second?

alarm, Spanish; beach, Roman M; Conservative, past events; considers, it seems to me

| Test Ten | COMPUTER ANIMALS | Question 4 |
|---|---|---|

Why might a computer user have a rodent, a ruminant, and a reptile?

Where can you find (in one place) collections of the following:

tools, organs, gems and weapons

What is the connection between the following?

1. hypersonic rocket-plane
2. pods of equipment
3. spaceship
4. submarine
5. space-station

What is the European connection with the following?

a train; more; pairs; solo

What links the names of the capitals of Gabon and Sierra Leone?

Which is the odd one out, and why?

Bingo, Bitchu, Bungo, Bango

| Test Ten | POETIC | Question 10 |

Which South Wales Valleys' town is a poetic contraction for 'below'?

| Test Ten | 3 LETTER LINK | Question 11 |

What is the three-letter connection between waterways in the UK, and firearms in the US?

| Test Ten | LIVING FISH | Question 12 |

How much whiskey is needed to keep a fish alive?

| Test Ten | COMMON | Question 13 |

What do the following have in common?

chess, king, queen, domino, green, moss, holly, berry

| Test Ten | SECOND SUNDAY | Question 14 |

If the first day of the month and the last day of the month are both a Monday, what takes place on the second Sunday of the month?

| Test Ten | INSERTED HYPHEN | Question 15 |

How does inserting a hyphen into 'brought under a trade organisation's rules' produce 'not charged'?

| Test Ten | SPORTS TEAMS | Question 16 |
|---|---|---|

What sequence does the following list represent?

beach volleyball, track relay race, basketball, ice hockey, netball, tug-of-war, baseball, lacrosse

| Test Ten | COLOURED WORD | Question 17 |
|---|---|---|

What six-letter word has its letters coloured as follows?

blue, red, yellow, blue, green, red

| Test Ten | SAVAGE | Question 18 |
|---|---|---|

Which Swiftian, vile, savage hominid was the first large-scale web directory?

| Test Ten | CONNECTION | Question 19 |
|---|---|---|

What is the connection between the following?

formula translation, beginner's all-purpose symbolic instruction code, common business oriented language

| Test Ten | DOUBLE YES | Question 20 |
|---|---|---|

What type of board is composed of two European words for 'Yes'?

| Test Ten | HOMPOHONES | Question 21 |
|---|---|---|

Which two homophones give rise to the following?

mythological river, out of town, Winnie the Pooh game

| Test Ten | FOUR BY THE BARD | Question 22 |

Name four plays by William Shakespeare with 'and' in the title.

| Test Ten | THREE MONTHS | Question 23 |

There are three consecutive months of the year that have a strong connection (independent of anything to do with the calendar). Which are they and why?

| Test Ten | MUSICAL TRANSLATION | Question 24 |

Which musical instrument can also be an item of stationery in one foreign language and a braggart, a spring flower, or a gangster's weapon in another?

| Test Ten | COMMON FEATURE | Question 25 |

What have the following in common?

elbow, moth, cobweb, pinch, snug

| Test Ten | LINK | Question 26 |

What single word links Frederic Dannay, Manfred B Lee, Farrokh Bulsara and Beatrix Armgard?

| Test Ten | ODD ONE OUT | Question 27 |

Which of the following is the odd one out?

butter, chocolate, float, pudding, run, shake, tooth

| Test Ten | SILENT S | Question 28 |
|---|---|---|

Which singular noun, from the French for abstract or summary, contains just one letter S (which is silent), but has an 'S' sound elsewhere?

| Test Ten | ODD ONE OUT | Question 29 |
|---|---|---|

Which of the following is the odd one out?

caribou, fox, hare, Inuit, lemming, musk ox, penguin, tree, tundra, wolf

| Test Ten | HOMOPHONES | Question 30 |
|---|---|---|

Which place names in the Outer Hebrides and in Sussex are derived from homophones?

| Test Ten | COMMON PEOPLE | Question 31 |
|---|---|---|

What do the following have in common?

Reg Dwight, Harry Webb, Maurice Micklewhite, Barry Pincus, Eleanore Fagan, George O'Dowd

| Test Ten | PREFIX | Question 32 |
|---|---|---|

Which word, when prefixed with 'un-', means exactly the same as before?

| Test Ten | SUFFIX | Question 33 |
|---|---|---|

Which two words, which mean the same, when given the suffix '-er' become opposites?

| Test Ten | NOT TWINS | Question 34 |
| --- | --- | --- |

Tom and George were born at the same hour on the same day to the same mother in the same hospital. They have the same father and yet they are not twins. Why?

| Test Ten | ODD ONE OUT | Question 35 |
| --- | --- | --- |

Which is the odd one out?

grandfather, sibling, brother-in-law, mother, aunt

| Test Ten | EURO HOMOPHONES | Question 36 |
| --- | --- | --- |

Which two European countries have homophones for a beverage with milk, and a cry of excited approval?

| Test Ten | EXTRA VOWEL | Question 37 |
| --- | --- | --- |

How does appending a vowel to a narcotic produce a homophone, meaning a leading lady?

| Test Ten | DIFFERENT NUMBERS | Question 38 |
| --- | --- | --- |

What is the connection between the numbers 1–10 and the following sequence?

1, 2, 3, 2, 1, 2, 3, 4, 2, 1       (Clue: think of the numbers expressed in a different way.)

| Test Ten | COMMON WORDS | Question 39 |
| --- | --- | --- |

What do the following words have in common?

era, devil, golf, part, spot, star, time, tram

| Test Ten | ADDING A LETTER | Question 40 |

What single letter can be added to each of the six following above to produce six new words?

rage, sack, beds, area, gash, bore

| Test Ten | FIND THE PHRASE | Question 41 |

A well-known phrase has had its initial letters and word boundaries removed. What is the phrase?

AKESEAD

| Test Ten | LINKING WORD | Question 42 |

Which word links: a quadrilateral, the BSI (British Standards Institute) and a bird of prey?

| Test Ten | NAME LINK | Question 43 |

What is the connection between the Egyptian (1922– present) former UN Secretary-General and the English writer (1873–1939) who was responsible for *The English* and *Transatlantic Review*, and the novel *The Good Soldier*?

| Test Ten | AUTHOR LINK | Question 44 |

What is the connection between the names of certain novels by the following authors?

Ray Bradbury; Arthur C Clarke; Joseph Heller; Dodie Smith; Sue Townshend

| Test Ten | ANIMAL | Question 45 |

Which animal fits the following?

dice roll; inefficacious product; treacherous

| Test Ten | ODD NAME OUT | Question 46 |

Which of these is the odd one out, and why? (Clue: famous names.)

Austerlitz, Bled, Konigsberg, Kappelhoff

| Test Ten | COMMON COMPOSITION | Question 47 |

What do the following musical compositions have in common?

Haydn's Toy Symphony, J.S. Bach's 'Bist du bei mir', Mozart's 'Adelaide' Concerto, Handel's Viola Concerto, Pergolesi's 'Concerti Armonici', Pugnani's Praeludium and Allegro?

| Test Ten | COUNTRY CONNECTION | Question 48 |

What country connects Buchinski and Kuryakin?

| Test Ten | ANATOMY | Question 49 |

Which part of a vertebrate's anatomy is comprised of eight bones connected by immovable joints?

| Test Ten | ALGORITHM | Question 50 |

What algorithm, when applied to the name of the errant computer in *2001 – A Space Odyssey*, produces a large computer company?

| Test Ten | HOMOPHONES | Question 51 |

Which two homophones link the following?

Ethiopia, Jamaica, a cathode-ray tube (TV screen) picture

| Test Ten | RELAXED TROUT | Question 52 |

Why do partridges become nervous while trout relax in September?

| Test Ten | COMMON NUMBERS | Question 53 |

What do the following numbers have in common?

25.4, 2.54, 0.3048, 0.9144, 1.6093

| Test Ten | UNIQUE | Question 54 |

What makes 7 and W unique among the numbers 1–10 and letters of the alphabet respectively?

| Test Ten | CONTAINED | Question 55 |

What do the following four words contain:

regretfully, probing, intravenous, knowledge

| Test Ten | LARGEST NUMBER | Question 56 |

In what way is 77 the largest number under 100?

| Test Ten | 2050 | Question 57 |

What applies to 2010 and 2050 which will not apply to any intervening year?

| Test Ten | FAMOUS? | Question 58 |

Who were the following?

1. Iosif Vissarionovich Dzhugashvili
2. Vladimir Ilyich Ulyanov
3. Aleksey Maksimovich Peshkov
4. Lev Davidovich Bronstein

| Test Ten | MISSING WORD | Question 59 |

Which word is missing from the solutions to the following clues?

a cutting tool
a fish
a group of animals
a soft fabric

| Test Ten | HOPE AND CROSBY | Question 60 |

Which word might describe the jaunty progress of Hope & Crosby?

| Test Ten | CONNECTION | Question 61 |

What connects the following?

Moliere, Voltaire, Boz, Twain

| Test Ten | REFERENCE | Question 62 |

To what do the following refer?

shrewdness, cowardice, skulk, consortium, crash

| Test Ten | WORDS AND NUMBERS | Question 63 |

Can you match these words and numbers – and why?

Coral, ivory, china, tin, paper

1, 10, 14, 20, 35

| Test Ten | PLACE NAME | Question 64 |

What is the place-name connection between the following?

original atomic bomb development, whisky and vermouth mixture, Woody Allen film

| Test Ten | GLOBAL | Question 65 |

What is the global significance of the following names?

Vittoria, Pelican, Golden Hind

| Test Ten | ACTING SCHOOL | Question 66 |

How does appending right to an acting school produce a form of electronic surveillance?

| Test Ten | ODD ONE OUT | Question 67 |

Which of the following is the odd one out?

crescent, full, gibbous, half, harvest, new

| Test Ten | ANIMALS | Question 68 |

Which animals are being described?

anguine, anserine, apian, murine

| Test Ten | UNIQUE TEMPERATURES | Question 69 |

Why are the Fahrenheit temperatures 61 and 82 unique?

| Test Ten | LATIN | Question 70 |

Regarding anglicisation, what do the following Latin or Italian words have in common?

agenda, candelabra, insignia, opera, panini

---

**DID YOU KNOW?**

Zerah Colburn was born in Vermont, USA, in 1840 and at the age of eight demonstrated a remarkable ability for the mental multiplication of powers. At London in 1848 Zerah raised 8 to the 16th power, the answer being: 241,474,976,710,656. Meanwhile as a further tremendous demonstration of mental powers, Mirat Arikan (born 1973) calculated the 39th root of an arbitrarily chosen 100-digit number in just 39 seconds. This took place in Istanbul, Turkey, in 1996.

Which name connects the following:

Edwards (film producer), William (artist, poet), Peter (painter)

Which is the odd one out?

uxoricide, parricide, vaticide

What is five times a jeroboam?

What do taghairm, bletonism and spodomancy have in common?

In a games context, what links David, Alexander, Caesar and Charlemagne?

Which is the odd one out?

affretttando, arpeggiare, spumante, forzando, smorzando

Pair up the following correctly:

da Vinci, Michaelangelo, Raphael, Botticelli
*The School of Athens, The Last Judgement, Mona Lisa, The Birth of Venus*

Name the more common terms for

calcium carbonate
nitrous oxide
sodium chloride
hydrated ferric oxide

What connection do the following words have with climate?

sown, Iran, steel, what, forts, mire

What word links the following?

Hungarian/US nuclear scientist, bank clerk, raconteur

What links these numbers?

39, 150, 27, 66

| Test Ten | BODY PARTS | Question 82 |
|---|---|---|

If aural means of the ear and cardiac means of the heart what do brachial, buccal and genal refer to?

| Test Ten | ACRONYMS | Question 83 |
|---|---|---|

The abbreviations DVD, RAM and RAM are now part of the language, but do you know what they stand for?

| Test Ten | IN COMMON | Question 84 |
|---|---|---|

What do Marengo, Copenhagen and Surrey have in common?

| Test Ten | CARS | Question 85 |
|---|---|---|

Which of these is the odd one out?

Ford, Jaguar, Lotus, Rover, Vauxhall

| Test Ten | YOUNG ANIMALS | Question 86 |
|---|---|---|

Of what animals are these the young?

elver, leveret, squab, joey

| Test Ten | 25 YEARS | Question 87 |
|---|---|---|

What is special about the 25-year sequence 1988–2012?

When was the last previous similar sequence of 25 or more years?

What is noteworthy about the following pairs of proverbs which have gone into common English usage?

si vis pacem, para bellum
vade in pace

tout comprendre c'est tout pardonner
nec scire fas est omnia

Put the following in order: smallest to largest

decare, hectare, centiare, acre

Which animals are referred to by these words?

apian, corvine, leporine, psittacine

Link the following diameters – in miles – with the appropriate planets

3,030, 7,500, 4,215, 74,500, 31,000

Saturn, Mercury, Neptune, Mars, Venus

| Test Ten | BAD SHOT | Question 93 |

Which amateur golfer's ball landed furthest from the green than any other in the history of the sport?

| Test Ten | TWICE AS LONG | Question 94 |

Where is tin twice as long as wood and china twice as long as tin?

| Test Ten | ANIMAL LINK | Question 95 |

Which animal (and its variants) links the following?

rocky movie, William Blake poem, A. A. Milne character

| Test Ten | RHYMING CONNECTION | Question 96 |

What is the rhyming connection between the following?

early Goon; tooth part; unsaturated hydrocarbon, comprising five carbon atoms

| Test Ten | MISSING NUMBERS | Question 97 |

What two numbers are missing from this sequence?

1, 1, 2, 6, 6, 12, ???, ???, 72, 216

| Test Ten | FEEL THE BEAT | Question 98 |

How many semihemidemisemiquavers make a quaver in music?

What is disastrous about the following numbers?

1,348, 1,665, 1,666, 1,756

What is this and what does it mean?

citius, altius, fortius

**Test One; Answer 1**
Isthmus.

**Test One; Answer 2**
6 (each horizontal row has two numbers that are half the other two).

**Test One; Answer 3**
7 (add the numbers top right and top left and divide by three).

**Test One; Answer 4**
6. Number of letters in the days of the week, starting Monday.

**Test One; Answer 5**
Oct. For example, triplets, sextuplets, quadruplets and octuplets.

**Test One; Answer 6**
229. The differences between progressive pairs of numbers are 15, 30, 60 and so 120 is added to 109 to give the final number.

**Test One; Answer 7**
125. Successive numbers are obtained by adding 1, 3, 9, 27. The next number in this sequence (the numbers are powers of 3) is 81. 44 + 81 = 125.

**Test One; Answer 8**
104. Successive numbers are obtained by adding 0, 1, 8, 27. The next number in this sequence (the numbers are cubes, i.e. $0^3 = 0$, $1^3 = 1$, $2^3 = 8$, $3^3 = 27$) is 64. 40 + 64 = 104.

**Test One; Answer 9**
Tony. Labour party leaders: Harold Wilson, James Callaghan, Michael Foot, Neil Kinnock, John Smith and Tony Blair.

**Test One; Answer 10**
Only Woktu is bogus, the rest are genuine.

**Test One; Answer 11**
ALPHA = 27 and OMEGA = 19. (G = 0, E = 1, L = 2, O = 3, T = 4, P = 5, A = 6, I = 7, H = 8, M = 9.)

**Test One; Answer 12**
7 + 478 + 673 + 9,095 = 10,253.

**Test One; Answer 13**
Conduction.

**Test One; Answer 14**
Polyphemus is the one-eyed cyclops, Sleipnir was the eight-legged horse of Wotan, Shelob is the monster spider in the Lord of the Rings (eight legs), The Kraken is a giant ten-tentacled squid and the giant Briareos had 100 arms.

**Test One; Answer 15**
216. The two previous numbers are multiplied together and the result divided by 2. The answer 156 is a justifiable alternative to 216, since the sequence increases each time by successive factorials: 1 (1!), 2 (2!), 6 (3!), 24 (4!), with the next being 120 (5!), giving 36 + 120 = 156.

**Test One; Answer 16**
a) SURGEON; b) ASTRONOMER.

**Test One; Answer 17**
142,857 × 3 = 428,571.

**Test One; Answer 18**
E: Initial letters of <u>O</u>ne to <u>E</u>ight.

**Test One; Answer 19**
29. The number is reached through the sum of alpha position (A = 1, B = 2, C = 3 etc) first letter plus the square of alpha position for the second letter. Thus T = 20 and C = 3; $20 + 3^2 = 29$.

**Test One; Answer 20**
Adieu and Audio.

**Test One; Answer 21**
```
   957
 + 528
 ----
 1,485
```

**Test One; Answer 22**
Marmoset.

**Test One; Answer 23**
Wednesday, sum of alpha position (A = 1, B = 2, C = 3 etc).

**Test One; Answer 24**
a) Jasper; b) Myrtle; c) Basil (herb); d) Louis.

**Test One; Answer 25**
Noel!

**Test One; Answer 26**
Water ($H_2O$).

**Test One; Answer 27**
The ages are 25, 4 and 2. These sum to 31, as do 20, 10 and 1 (the product of which is also 200). This is why the census taker needs the extra information. It can be deduced that the number of the house is 31 since this is the only number that requires the census taker to seek further information.

**Test One; Answer 28**
Whales. Gaggle and Pod are the appropriate collective nouns in each instance.

**Test One; Answer 29**
AND = 498. Each new word adds one to the original value of a letter.

**Test One; Answer 30**
Murder. Murder and Pride are the appropriate collective nouns in each instance.

**Test One; Answer 31**
5,325 and also –5,325. Two negative numbers multiplied together always yield a positive result.

**Test One; Answer 32**
Ball.

**Test One; Answer 33**
Macbeth called the witches jugging fiends.

**Test One; Answer 34**
No. The act of catching a falling object exerts sufficient force to destroy the bridge.

**Test One; Answer 35**
8, 5, 4, 9, 1, 7, 6, 3, 2. The numbers are placed in alphabetical order (eight, five, four, nine, one, seven, six, three and two).

**Test One; Answer 36**
Turn switch one on and wait ten minutes. Then turn switch one off, turn switch two on and enter the room. One lamp will be lit, corresponding to switch two. Now feel the other two lamps – the hot bulb will be connected to switch one and the cold one to switch three.

**Test One; Answer 37**
DAH. Replace each letter with its alphabetical position and the sums will then make sense.

**Test One; Answer 38**
V. All the letters have an 'EE' sound when spoken.

**Test One; Answer 39**
G. The letters are the initials of colours. Red and Yellow mixed together give Orange, Blue and Red give Purple and Yellow and Blue give Green.

**Test One; Answer 40**
11. The previous two numbers are added each time to give the next number.

**Test One; Answer 41**
SAVIOUR and VARIOUS.

**Test One; Answer 42**
234. The alphabetical position of the first and last letter in each name are multiplied.

**Test One; Answer 43**
FEWER. It is not a palindrome (a word that reads the same forwards as backwards).

**Test One; Answer 44**
50p.

**Test One; Answer 45**
SPRING, SUMMER, AUTUMN, WINTER.

**Test One; Answer 46**
49. In each name the first Roman numeral minus the last Roman numeral gives the age. (C – L = 50; L – V = 45; V – I = 4; L – I = 49.)

**Test One; Answer 47**
J. (January, February, March, April, May, June.)

**Test One; Answer 48**
Chloe has 7 sweets and Sam 13.

**Test One; Answer 49**
T.S. Eliot, Dryden, Milton, Shakespeare.

**Test One; Answer 50**
Shakespeare. Trinculo in *The Tempest*.

**Test One; Answer 51**
They are geological periods, the most recent being: CRETACEOUS followed by JURASSIC, TRIASSIC and CARBONIFEROUS.

**Test One; Answer 52**
William Blake, *Songs of Experience*, 'The Tyger'.

**Test One; Answer 53**
Lady Macbeth in Shakespeare's *Macbeth* from the speech 'Is this a dagger I see before me?'

**Test One; Answer 54**
4. If two consecutive numbers in the first row are added and the result halved, the number below is generated. For example, $(35 + 37)/2 = 36$. This gives the answer $(5 + 3)/2 = 4$.

**Test One; Answer 55**
Neptune 8; Jupiter 16; Uranus 15; Saturn 18. The number of moons orbiting each planet.

**Test One; Answer 56**
Mercury 0.2408; Venus 0.6152; Mars 1.881; Pluto 248.5. Planetary years expressed in earth years as the basic unit.

**Test One; Answer 57**
Hydrogen 1, Helium 2, Lithium 3, Carbon 6, Oxygen 8 – these being the atomic numbers of the substances.

**Test One; Answer 58**
Pluto – Charon; Saturn – Titan; Uranus – Miranda; Mars – Phobos; Jupiter – Io; Neptune – Triton. The planets are matched with one of their moons.

**Test One; Answer 59**
Harrison. Rex Harrison played Professor Higgins and Dr Doolittle, while Harrison Ford played Han Solo and Indiana Jones.

**Test One; Answer 60**
Pooh in A.A. Milne's *Winnie the Pooh*.

**Test One; Answer 61**
3.5 pounds.

**Test One; Answer 62**
Alice in Lewis Carroll's *Alice in Wonderland*. (Lewis Carroll was the pseudonym of Charles Lutwidge Dodgson.)

**Test One; Answer 63**
$10^{28}$.

**Test One; Answer 64**
Neuron.

**Test One; Answer 65**
*The Adventures of Sherlock Holmes* by Sir Arthur Conan Doyle, in the story 'The Five Orange Pips'.

**Test One; Answer 66**
II. Twentieth century British monarchs Edward VII, George V, Edward VIII, George VI, Elizabeth II.

**Test One; Answer 67**
LIFE OF BRIAN – cinematography; CAMBRIAN – geology; ELGIN MARBLES – classical Greek statues; MANUBRIUM – osteology.

**Test One; Answer 68**
20. b1–h8 is 5 moves, b6 to g1 is 4 moves.

**Test One; Answer 69**
Hydrogen 1, Carbon 12, Nitrogen 14, Oxygen 16, Helium 4.

**Test One; Answer 70**
Falstaff in Shakespeare's *King Henry IV, Part II*.

**Test One; Answer 71**
Lord Byron in 'English Bards and Scotch Reviewers'.

**Test One; Answer 72**
36. The planets are ranked as to their distance from the sun (Jupiter is 5, Mercury is 1 and Pluto 9).

**Test One; Answer 73**
Lady Macbeth in Shakespeare's *Macbeth*.

**Test One; Answer 74**
8. The names represent the total number of kings with that name (Richard III, Stephen – only one – and Charles II).

**Test One; Answer 75**
African Studies – NAIROBI; Middle Eastern Studies – BAHRAIN; Modern Cartoon Techniques – DAN BLAIR; Latin American Studies – BUENOS AIRES.

**Test One; Answer 76**
Number A – 102,564; Number B – 410,256.

**Test One; Answer 77**
Wellington – Waterloo; Cardigan – Balaklava; Caesar – Alesia; Kutuzov – Borodino; Marlborough – Blenheim.

**Test One; Answer 78**
A goes with B (5 mins); B comes back (with the light – 10 mins); C goes with D (30 mins); A comes back (31 mins); A goes with B (36 mins).

**Test One; Answer 79**
Evolution, Catastrophism, Santa Maria, Argo.

**Test One; Answer 80**
1326. Dates of accession to the throne, averaged out.

**Test One; Answer 81**
Titus.

**Test One; Answer 82**
The maximum possible is 8. One solution is a4, b6, c8, d2, e7, f1, g3 and h5.

**Test One; Answer 83**
Frederick John Perry was a tennis champion. Matthew Perry was the US Naval Commander who opened relations with Japan. Perry Mason was a fictional lawyer, Perry White is editor of the *Daily Planet* in the Superman series and 'The Peer and the Peri' is the subtitle to the Gilbert and Sullivan opera *Iolanthe*.

**Test One; Answer 84**
22, 23 and 35. We factor 17,710: 2, 5, 7, 11, 23. This is the unique breakdown in the prime factors. Then the only way to get three numbers, each bigger than 19 is 2 × 11 = 22; 5 × 7 = 35 and 23 left over.

**Test One; Answer 85**
Acacia. The wildebeest is the prime element of the lion's diet as the acacia is for the giraffe.

**Test One; Answer 86**
5 and 17. They are all prime numbers. The answer is 9,699,690.

**Test One; Answer 87**
Nelson – Aboukir; Themistocles – Salamis; Howard – The Armada; Howe – Ushant; Don John – Lepanto. Naval commanders and their victories.

**Test One; Answer 88**
6. One more than the total number of colours.

**Test One; Answer 89**
AARDVARK.

**Test One; Answer 90**
Athlete 3.

**Test One; Answer 91**
138, 276. The numbers either increase by 6 or double.

**Test One; Answer 92**
Waterloo. The military career of both commanders was finished at the respective battles.

**Test One; Answer 93**
112, 105. The numbers alternately increase by 9 or decrease by 7.

**Test One; Answer 94**
No navel. (Adam was created and not born.)

**Test One; Answer 95**
X = 44.

**Test One; Answer 96**
Item A costs $47, B costs $51. You purchase C for $63 and have $17 change.

**Test One; Answer 97**
John.

**Test One; Answer 98**
11 hours.

**Test One; Answer 99**
C, A, B, D, E.

**Test One; Answer 100**
Mama bear.

## TEST TWO SOLUTIONS

**Test Two; Answer 1**
32.

**Test Two; Answer 2**
Staunton £480; Barleycorn £400; Lewis £160; Russian £560.

**Test Two; Answer 3**
1,200 euros.

**Test Two; Answer 4**
Total bill £513. The chairman should have paid £156 and the Vice President should have paid £192.

**Test Two; Answer 5**
Six – the size of the sets is irrelevant!

**Test Two; Answer 6**
200 guests, 300 members.

**Test Two; Answer 7**
Colonel 'B's wife.

**Test Two; Answer 8**
Hypoteneuse is a feature of a triangle, the others are features of a circle.

**Test Two; Answer 9**
The set cost £100.50, while the replacement piece cost 50p.

**Test Two; Answer 10**
Brunnhilde would have been its great aunt and Sleipnir its great uncle.

**Test Two; Answer 11**
Do you spell your name with a 'V', Mr Wagner?

**Test Two; Answer 12**
300,000 kilometres.

**Test Two; Answer 13**
Albert.

**Test Two; Answer 14**
Bilbo Baggins – Smaug the Dragon; Frodo Baggins – Shelob the Spider; Hercules – The Lernean Hydra; Captain Nemo – The Giant Squid; Beowulf – Grendel.

**Test Two; Answer 15**
$a = 23$, $b = 69$, $c = 200$. $a + c - b = 154$.

**Test Two; Answer 16**
Wellington – Copenhagen; Alexander the Great – Bucephalus; Caligula – Incitatus; Wotan – Sleipnir; Perseus – Pegasus.

**Test Two; Answer 17**
$a = 12$ or $3$ (either double or half the above number); $b = 7$. Therefore $(12 + 3) \times 7 = 105$.

**Test Two; Answer 18**
Saqqara – The Step Pyramid; Rhodes – The Colossus; Athens – The Parthenon; Moscow – The Kremlin; Washington – The Lincoln Memorial; Olympia – Temple of Zeus.

**Test Two; Answer 19**
$a = 46$ (the sequence is the square numbers, but with the double digits reversed: $8 \times 8 = 64$); $b = 45$ (the sequence increases alternately by 2 and 10). Therefore $46 - 45 = 1$.

**Test Two; Answer 20**
Rameses II – Kadesh; Antony and Cleopatra – Actium; Hermann – Teutoberger Forest; Leonidas – Thermopylae; Ulysses S Grant – The Wilderness.

**Test Two; Answer 21**
A fool and his money are soon parted.

**Test Two; Answer 22**
364.

**Test Two; Answer 23**
260.

**Test Two; Answer 24**
38 groats and 7 pfennigs.

**Test Two; Answer 25**
19 groats and 88 pfennigs.

**Test Two; Answer 26**
The sequence is Phobos (Mars), Io (Jupiter), Titan (Saturn), Titania (Neptune) and Charon (Pluto).

**Test Two; Answer 27**
As Commander Data would put it: it is 'a pursuit of undomesticated fowl' (a wild goose chase), since neither planet has any moons.

**Test Two; Answer 28**
a) Marston Moor (1644) × Naseby (1645) = 2,704,380; b) Agincourt (1415) + Hastings (1066) = 2,481.

**Test Two; Answer 29**
The Twelve Labours of Hercules; The Nine Muses; The Three Graces; The 24 Books of Homer's *Iliad*.

**Test Two; Answer 30**
2.

**Test Two; Answer 31**
6.

**Test Two; Answer 32**
150,000.

**Test Two; Answer 33**
31.

**Test Two; Answer 34**
One million (1,000 × 1,000).

**Test Two; Answer 35**
927.

**Test Two; Answer 36**
606 (600 + 6).

**Test Two; Answer 37**
The answer 'No!' creates a win–win situation for Sir Galahad. If the Guardian proves him wrong by letting him across, he has achieved his goal. If the Guardian says that Sir Galahad's answer is right then he must allow him across the bridge, because he has given the right answer.

**Test Two; Answer 38**
Pond, lake, sea. H2O is water.

**Test Two; Answer 39**
A further 22 hours and 30 minutes.

**Test Two; Answer 40**
White. The bear is sitting on the North Pole which is due north of all other points.

**Test Two; Answer 41**
Yes.

**Test Two; Answer 42**
Yes – if the source of the water is on the same level as the city, water will find its own level and can, therefore, run uphill.

**Test Two; Answer 43**
Picasso – the artist is the odd one out.

**Test Two; Answer 44**
Shakespeare – *Cymbeline*; Marlowe – *Tamberlaine*; Mozart – *Zauberflöte*; Milton – *Paradise Lost*.

**Test Two; Answer 45**
119.

**Test Two; Answer 46**
Pour the contents from three into six and return three to its original position.

**Test Two; Answer 47**
5,049.

**Test Two; Answer 48**
Yes. If the number of goblins exceeds the number of possible wrinkles then there must be two goblins with the same number.

**Test Two; Answer 49**
£2,000.

**Test Two; Answer 50**
Speed is irrelevant. When they meet they are both the same distance from P.

**Test Two; Answer 51**
They all mean 'two', respectively in Russian, French, German, Italian and Spanish.

**Test Two; Answer 52**
10%.

**Test Two; Answer 53**
Kant, Plato, Aristotle and Wittgenstein are all fine, but Rubens was a painter.

**Test Two; Answer 54**
4 times.

**Test Two; Answer 55**
EINSTEIN – RELATIVITY; DODGSON (Lewis Carroll) – LOOKING GLASS; GOETHE – FAUST; NEWTON – GRAVITY; GATES – MICROSOFT.

**Test Two; Answer 56**
He takes the rabbit across, as the cat will not eat the carrots. He returns alone and then takes the cat across. He then returns with the rabbit and takes the carrots across. Finally, he comes back alone to collect the rabbit.

**Test Two; Answer 57**
AUSTRALIA – CANBERRA; DENMARK – COPENHAGEN; AUSTRIA – VIENNA; S. KOREA – SEOUL; FINLAND – HELSINKI.

**Test Two; Answer 58**
3. Shift A to the mid-point beneath H and I, shift G and J to either side of B and C.

**Test Two; Answer 59**
A, A, B, B.

**Test Two; Answer 60**
M or 1000.

**Test Two; Answer 61**
14 and 12 between 6 and 2; 18 and 10 between 2 and 4; 16 and 8 between 6 and 4.

**Test Two; Answer 62**
The 5th Indian clockwise or anti-clockwise to the chief.

**Test Two; Answer 63**
'Tough', 'women' and 'station' show how 'fish' could be justified.

**Test Two; Answer 64**
On the analogy of 'ghoti': gnash, honest, people, mortgage and friend, the word 'ghoti' might not even be pronounceable.

**Test Two; Answer 65**
54.

**Test Two; Answer 66**
MERCURY, VENUS, EARTH, MARS, JUPITER, SATURN. The large object is the sun.

**Test Two; Answer 67**
6 (32 minus 26).

**Test Two; Answer 68**
The tank regiment.

**Test Two; Answer 69**
BULL is to COW as STAG is to DOE.

**Test Two; Answer 70**
11.

**Test Two; Answer 71**
The cold tap rate is 600/30 = 20 litres per minute. The hot tap rate is 600/40 = 15 litres per minute. The rate of emptying is 600/50 = 12 litres per minute. Therefore the total amount of water coming in is 35 litres per minute. 12 litres are leaving the bath every minute. So the rate of the bath filling is 23 litres per minute. So 600/23 = 26.09 mins.

**Test Two; Answer 72**
Nonsense.

**Test Two; Answer 73**
Richard = 6 and Charles = 3. The numbers of the English monarchs are added together, thus Richard I, II and III = 6.

**Test Two; Answer 74**
Casa Rosada – General Galtieri; The Kremlin – Boris Yeltsin; The White House – Bill Clinton; 10 Downing Street – Tony Blair.

**Test Two; Answer 75**
30 hours. Team A completes one hyperdrive and three torpedo armings. Team B completes two sets of hyperdrive.

**Test Two; Answer 76**
Neither of them!

**Test Two; Answer 77**
5 miles. If he starts towards the North Pole and continues beyond it in a straight line he continues from north to south without changing course.

**Test Two; Answer 78**
They filled the 500 gallon container and used that to fill the 300 one. The residue is 200 gallons. Do this twice and you have 400 gallons.

**Test Two; Answer 79**
20,000.

**Test Two; Answer 80**
Surprisingly, the answer is not the intuitive 600 mph but 583.33 mph. For example if the plane travels 100 miles, the outward leg takes 8.57 minutes and the return leg 12 minutes. Total travel time is therefore 20.57 minutes, which equates to an average speed of 583.33 mph.

**Test Two; Answer 81**
They exchange horses.

**Test Two; Answer 82**
6.

**Test Two; Answer 83**
His 99th.

**Test Two; Answer 84**
Hannibal – Elephants; T.S. Eliot – Cats; Hemingway – Big Game; Darwin – Apes.

**Test Two; Answer 85**
A: 4 in 7; B: 2 in 7; C: 1 in 7.

**Test Two; Answer 86**
The four possible solutions are:

a) X + I = II. The left hand side is in Roman numerals, while the right hand side is in our number system (i.e. 10 + 1 = 11).

b) Moving a matchstick from the right hand side, and placing it next to the 'V' creates a square root sign. The equation then reads: the square root of +1 = 1.

c) Moving the vertical matchstick from the plus sign to create 'IV' on the right hand side gives: V – I = IV.

d) On of the matchsticks from the right hand side of the equation can be used to create a 'not equals to' sign instead of an equals sign.

**Test Two; Answer 87**
Intaglio.

**Test Two; Answer 88**
All are collective nouns: Lions, Ravens and Crows respectively.

**Test Two; Answer 89**
Cheshire – Cat; Whittington – Mayor; Archer – Sherwood; Stilton – Cheese.

**Test Two; Answer 90**
INDIVISIBILITY or TARAMASALATA.

**Test Two; Answer 91**
ABSTEMIOUS, FACETIOUS, CAESIOUS.

**Test Two; Answer 92**
UNNOTICEABLY, SUBCONTINENTAL, UNCOMPLIMENTARY.

**Test Two; Answer 93**
Make three sets of three and balance any one set against any other. The heavy ball will then be revealed as being in one of these sets or, if they balance, in the set not weighed. Taking the set identified and then repeating the procedure with two individual balls from this set, reveals the heavier ball.

**Test Two; Answer 94**
Answer to the nearest second = 5 minutes and 27 seconds after 7am.

**Test Two; Answer 95**
£51. Add up all three prices and divide by 2.

**Test Two; Answer 96**
The landlord of the Pig and Whistle pub is complaining to a signwriter about a job: 'The spacing is all wrong,' he said. 'There's too much room between Pig and 'and', and 'and' and Whistle.'

**Test Two; Answer 97**
Yes. This improves your chances of being correct from one in three to two in three.

If this seems confusing, consider the problem as follows: If you do not change your choice, you will only win if your original guess was correct (one chance in three); if you *do* change your choice, you will always win if your original guess was wrong (two chances in three).

For example: Say the million is in 'c'. If you choose 'a', the host *has* to open 'b' (because he knows that 'c' contains the million) and the switch (to 'c') will be a winning move. Similarly, if you choose 'b' the host *has* to open 'a', and again the switch (to 'c') will win. Of course if you choose 'c' and switch then you lose. But the switch wins two times out of three.

**Test Two; Answer 98**
Battle of Waterloo – 1815; King Charles I executed – 1649; Battle of Hastings – 1066; Foundation of Rome – 753BC.

**Test Two; Answer 99**
4. (4 is the 'square' of 2.) There is actually an ingenious alternative solution: IL (Roman for 49 – the square of 7).

**Test Two; Answer 100**
A and B can, the rest cannot.

**Test Three; Answer 1**
3651.

**Test Three; Answer 2**
Bob, where Tom had had 'had', had had 'had had'; 'had had' had had the teacher's approval.

**Test Three; Answer 3**
10 pounds.

**Test Three; Answer 4**
10 minutes.

**Test Three; Answer 5**
Long time, no see (Century).

**Test Three; Answer 6**
October (because of the extra hour) in the Northern hemisphere. March in the Southern hemisphere.

**Test Three; Answer 7**
18. The numbers are square numbers in reverse: 4 squared is 16, 5 squared is 25, etc. 9 squared is 81, giving 18 as the answer.

**Test Three; Answer 8**
SNAIL, SNARL, SNARE, SHARE, SHALE, SHALL, SHELL.

**Test Three; Answer 9**
Cain.

**Test Three; Answer 10**
81. Everybody loses one match except the winner.

**Test Three; Answer 11**
30.

**Test Three; Answer 12**
Brian LARA. The Aral Sea.

**Test Three; Answer 13**
BACKFIRED, BOLDFACE, OBFUSCATED.

**Test Three; Answer 14**
Foreign-backed (as in foreign-backed troops).

**Test Three; Answer 15**
Abhors, almost, biopsy and chintz.

**Test Three; Answer 16**
The Tokyo Olympics were held in 1964.

**Test Three; Answer 17**
196 (rotation 961, swapped digits 169). There is an alternative solution: 100 (since the rotation 001 = 1).

**Test Three; Answer 18**
1558. Years when Tudor monarchs came to the throne (Henry VII, Henry VIII, Edward VI, Mary, Elizabeth I).

**Test Three; Answer 19**
676.

**Test Three; Answer 20**
77. Subsequent numbers are obtained by multiplying together the digits of the previous one (e.g. 7 × 7 = 49; 4 × 9 = 36).

**Test Three; Answer 21**
do – done, which is an anagram of 'odd one'.

**Test Three; Answer 22**
A cob is a male swan and the pen is the female.

**Test Three; Answer 23**
Over one thousand years ago – 28/8/888.

**Test Three; Answer 24**
The African grey parrot can acquire a substantial vocabulary, is said to recognise colours and shapes and has been described as having the IQ of a two year old.

**Test Three; Answer 25**
Swans. They are unusual in that they have three collective nouns. Flock on the ground, fleet on the water and flight in the air.

**Test Three; Answer 26**
64. (64 squared is 4096 which is also 16 cubed.)

**Test Three; Answer 27**
James Bond (007).

**Test Three; Answer 28**
6,889.

**Test Three; Answer 29**
If you make the largest possible number from the digits 6, 1, 7 and 4 and subtract the smallest, you end up back with 6,174, i.e. 7,641 − 1,467 = 6,174. If you try this procedure with any four-digit number you will, within seven steps, arrive at 6,174.

**Test Three; Answer 30**
Demeter. Neptune and Poseidon are the Roman and Greek gods of the sea. Ceres and Demeter are the same for the Goddess of cultivation.

**Test Three; Answer 31**
A Scrabble set. Each letter is used once and only once. The 'R' in 'dear' and the 'D' in 'and' are blanks.

**Test Three; Answer 32**
13. 13 squared is 169 and 31 squared is 961.

**Test Three; Answer 33**
'ough' is pronounced seven different ways.

**Test Three; Answer 34**
essayasse (from the verb essayer to try).

**Test Three; Answer 35**
The sentence is palindromic (reads the same forwards as backwards).

**Test Three; Answer 36**
Uncopyrightables.

**Test Three; Answer 37**
They are the final digits of successive square numbers (i.e. 1, 4, 9, 16 etc.).

**Test Three; Answer 38**
YHN. The three letter combinations are created by moving across the three rows of a keyboard from left to right.

**Test Three; Answer 39**
Exe, Wye, Dee, Tees and Severn all eventually end in sea.

**Test Three; Answer 40**
41; 27 September 1951 (note that 1992 is a leap year and that 41 × 271 = 11,111).

**Test Three; Answer 41**
Any point exactly 500 miles south of the equator. There is actually an ingenious alternative possibility: starting approximately 140 miles north of the South Pole, or starting approximately 1140 miles South of the North Pole.

**Test Three; Answer 42**
The South Pole or any point within 1,000 miles of the North Pole.

**Test Three; Answer 43**
Nothing else in the English Language rhymes with them.

**Test Three; Answer 44**
Tonic water.

**Test Three; Answer 45**
10 minutes later: 1805 = Battle of Trafalgar, 1815 = Battle of Waterloo.

**Test Three; Answer 46**
a) SS. French numbers = six, sept; b) SD. French days of the week = samedi, dimanche.

**Test Three; Answer 47**
Pack my box with five dozen liquor jugs.

**Test Three; Answer 48**
Catherine was born in 1972 and is 28. Note that it is also theoretically possible for Catherine to be 56 but, despite recent advances, 28 is a more common age to become a mother.

**Test Three; Answer 49**
They each contain three letters which are alphabetically contiguous, e.g. LMN, NOP, DEF etc.

**Test Three; Answer 50**
An ounce of gold. Gold is measured in troy weight and 1 ounce troy = 31.1035gms. Sugar is measured in avoirdupois weight and 1 ounce avoirdupois = 28.3495gms.

**Test Three; Answer 51**
5 (raised to the 5) + 4 (raised to the 5) + 7 (raised to the 5) + 4 (raised to the 5) + 8 (raised to the 5) = 54748.

**Test Three; Answer 52**
They are anagrams of one two, three four, five six, seven eight, nine ten, eleven twelve.

**Test Three; Answer 53**
E1GHT. Replace the numbers with Roman numerals as follows: (4 = IV, 9 = IX, 5 = V and 1 = I).

**Test Three; Answer 54**
Queueing (an acceptable spelling according to Chambers).

**Test Three; Answer 55**
40 degrees.

**Test Three; Answer 56**
Two complete revolutions (the width of the note is approximately 2.7 times the diameter of the 5p coin).

**Test Three; Answer 57**
Just over three feet (actually one foot × Pi).

**Test Three; Answer 58**
ELEVEN + TWO = TWELVE + ONE. The two sides are anagrams of each other. There is also a remarkable mathematical feature of this equation: 11 + 2 = 12 + 1 works in all bases above 2.

**Test Three; Answer 59**
If you count the letters, it gives the constant Pi to 15 digits: 3.14159265358979.

**Test Three; Answer 60**
St John's Wood.

**Test Three; Answer 61**
The famous Duke of Malborough who commanded the British army during the War of the Spanish succession won his most celebrated victories at Blenheim, Ramillies, Oudenarde and Malplaquet in 1704, 1706, 1708 and 1709.

**Test Three; Answer 62**
a) 5 minutes; b) 2,000 flies.

**Test Three; Answer 63**
They all comprise ten different letters of the alphabet.

**Test Three; Answer 64**
To accentuate the second letter and thus differentiate Iceland from Ireland, especially in Morse Code, where C is dash-dot-dash-dot and R is dot-dash-dot.

**Test Three; Answer 65**
Neither. They are yellow.

**Test Three; Answer 66**
Each word contains a word meaning 'nothing', e.g. naught, nil, love and duck.

**Test Three; Answer 67**
None. The sum of the digits is 45 which is divisible by 3. Any number which has this property will always be divisible by 3.

**Test Three; Answer 68**
Too wise you are, too wise you be, I see you are too wise for me.

**Test Three; Answer 69**
The first letter is as far from the end of the alphabet as the last letter is from the start (e.g. xenophobic: x is third from the end, c is third from the beginning).

**Test Three; Answer 70**
GATE, PATE, PATH, PASH, POSH, POOH, POOR, DOOR.

**Test Three; Answer 71**
SPARKLING: SPARKING, SPARING, SPRING, SPRIG, PRIG, PIG, PI, I.
STARTLING: STARTING, STARING, STRING, STING, SING, SIN, IN, I.

**Test Three; Answer 72**
ASPIRATED, SPIRATED, PIRATED, PIRATE, IRATE, RATE, RAT, AT, A.

CLEANSERS, CLEANSER, CLEANSE, CLEANS, CLEAN, LEAN, EAN, AN, A.

**Test Three; Answer 73**
1892, when they were 44, the year would be 1936 (= 44 squared). Note that those born in 1980 will be 45 in 2025 (= 45 squared).

**Test Three; Answer 74**
If the grate be empty put coal on. If the grate be full stop putting coal on.

**Test Three; Answer 75**
Catherine puts three sweets into each of three bags and then puts all three bags into the fourth bag.

**Test Three; Answer 76**
2100.

**Test Three; Answer 77**
September was originally the seventh month, October the eighth, November the ninth and December the tenth. All names refer to Latin numbers.

**Test Three; Answer 78**
Pea Green; Key Door; Sea Salt; Swans Fleet; Whales Pod; Locusts Swarm; Handel Concerto.

**Test Three; Answer 79**
Cacophonous.

**Test Three; Answer 80**
2 to the power of 64. 2 to the power of 64 minus 1 is the chessboard answer, but Dante writes 'surpass' and so one more is needed.

**Test Three; Answer 81**
Nine pounds.

**Test Three; Answer 82**
Two and five respectively. (The question refers to the number of bars or lines used to form digital numbers.)

**Test Three; Answer 83**
Bookkeeping.

**Test Three; Answer 84**
In the English language, E is the most frequently used letter, followed by T, A, O etc.

**Test Three; Answer 85**
Smile becomes Simile.

**Test Three; Answer 86**
155. Multiply the two preceding numbers and then add one, e.g. $(1 \times 2) + 1 = 3$, $(2 \times 3) + 1 = 7$ etc.

**Test Three; Answer 87**
Stop, spot, post, pots, tops, opts.

**Test Three; Answer 88**
2000. Times on a 24-hour clock.

**Test Three; Answer 89**
If you remove the first letter you are left with names of English rivers.

**Test Three; Answer 90**
Spring, summer, autumn and winter all have six letters. In French printemps (spring) is much longer than été (summer).

**Test Three; Answer 91**
rot, sort, tours, routes, rouster, courters, trouncers, recounters, intercourse, resurrection.

**Test Three; Answer 92**
P. The letters are the initials of the planets in order from the sun.

**Test Three; Answer 93**
Edgehill and Al Alamein, both on 23 October in 1642 and 1942 respectively.

**Test Three; Answer 94**
11 days were lost due to the calendar change in 1752.

**Test Three; Answer 95**
They are all misnomers: the ring-tailed cat is not a cat, the crayfish is not a fish etc.

**Test Three; Answer 96**
Buckfastleigh.

**Test Three; Answer 97**
Each is the only number in the language that has the same number of letters as its meaning.

**Test Three; Answer 98**
All the words are also French words.

**Test Three; Answer 99**
Two possible answers are: drapes, padres, parsed, rasped, spader, spared and spread or palest, pastel, petals, plates, pleats, septal and staple.

**Test Three; Answer 100**
BUSH, BASH, BASE, BARE, BORE, GORE.

## TEST FOUR SOLUTIONS

**Test Four; Answer 1**
Morse code.

**Test Four; Answer 2**
2,000. It is the next number that does not contain an 'e' in its spelling.

**Test Four; Answer 3**
House numbers for a front door.

**Test Four; Answer 4**
Beekeeper.

**Test Four; Answer 5**
All vowels occur only once in forward then reverse order.

**Test Four; Answer 6**
10.

**Test Four; Answer 7**
Senselessness.

**Test Four; Answer 8**
Stonechat, partridge, nuthatch and crossbill and all birds. Brimstone is a butterfly.

**Test Four; Answer 9**
Princes.

**Test Four; Answer 10**
They can all have any vowel put in the middle to make a word e.g. bag, beg, big, bog, bug.

**Test Four; Answer 11**
SIGHT-SCREEN, CATCH-PHRASE, WATCH-STRAP.

**Test Four; Answer 12**
Valuable – Invaluable.

**Test Four; Answer 13**
There are many possible answers, including A is Monday and B is Thursday.

**Test Four; Answer 14**
www – World Wide Web.

**Test Four; Answer 15**
An hourglass – because of all the sand.

**Test Four; Answer 16**
The resolution not to keep any resolutions.

**Test Four; Answer 17**
Knightsbridge.

**Test Four; Answer 18**
48 years.

**Test Four; Answer 19**
Replace each 'y' with 'port': 'Oporto is an important port in Portugal which exports port'.

**Test Four; Answer 20**
They are all units of measurement – respectively for horses, typefaces, length and diamonds.

**Test Four; Answer 21**
Until. Each word starts with the second letter of the previous word.

**Test Four; Answer 22**
All four representations are perfect squares: 441, 40401, 10404 and 144.

**Test Four; Answer 23**
They have four letters alphabetically in sequence and together.

**Test Four; Answer 24**
A letter (different in each case) can be added to make a new word with the same pronounciation: heArd, sCent, styE, reiGn, Hour, Knew, bUy, Wrest.

**Test Four; Answer 25**
S-N-O-W (the chemical symbols are Sn, O and W).

**Test Four; Answer 26**
En suite (onze huit).

**Test Four; Answer 27**
Columbus – America; Marlowe – Tamberlaine; Goethe – Faust; Gutenberg – Bible; da Vinci – Mona Lisa.

**Test Four; Answer 28**
Only the stupid ones, the rest have flown away.

**Test Four; Answer 29**
Deified.

**Test Four; Answer 30**
Semaphore.

**Test Four; Answer 31**
DUPUYTREN contains five consecutive letters in the reverse order that they appear on the typewriter keyboard. The only word to do so.

**Test Four; Answer 32**
It goes down slightly. The brick (being denser than water) takes up less volume of pool water than the weight of water it displaced when on the lilo.

**Test Four; Answer 33**
Pascal, Ole (Gunner Solskjaer), Ada, C and Oberon are all computer languages.

**Test Four; Answer 34**
A couple of feet or so. The third stomach of a ruminant can be known as a bible.

**Test Four; Answer 35**
212. They are the temperatures of boiling water on the four scales, Reamur, Celcius, Kelvin and Fahrenheit.

**Test Four; Answer 36**
A neighbouring farmer lent them a cow, making the total 18. One-half is now 9 cows, one-third is 6 cows and one-ninth 2 cows, making 17 in total. They divided the cattle and then returned the one left over to their neighbour.

**Test Four; Answer 37**
The men are grandfather, father and son.

**Test Four; Answer 38**
Alan puts a lock on the chest and sends it to Bill. Bill then puts his own lock on the chest and returns it to Alan. Alan removes his own lock and sends it back. Bill can then undo his own lock and remove the documents.

**Test Four; Answer 39**
The tip of the mast, as this created the biggest arc in traversing the globe.

**Test Four; Answer 40**
None. It is now winter.

**Test Four; Answer 41**
He is playing monopoly.

**Test Four; Answer 42**
Assassinate – no letters used twice, some three or four times, but none twice!

**Test Four; Answer 43**
50p. Press the random button. It won't be random and then you can work out the others.

**Test Four; Answer 44**
Start the timers together. When 4 has run out turn it over (4 mins) When 7 runs out turn that over (7 mins) When 4 has run out again (8 mins) turn over 7 again. Only one minute's worth of sand has gone through and so inverting it allows you to measure the final minute.

**Test Four; Answer 45**
He is a space-walking astronaut and his glove came off.

**Test Four; Answer 46**
Brown bread costs 50p and white bread 40p. The first man paid with a 50p piece, the second man used two 20p coins and one 10p coin.

**Test Four; Answer 47**
The first one. Water freezes at 32 degrees Fahrenheit.

**Test Four; Answer 48**
Neither – you are over water.

**Test Four; Answer 49**
87 – he's looking at the numbers upside down.

**Test Four; Answer 50**
The letters of his name are the initial letters of the months July to November, leaving seven months unrepresented.

**Test Four; Answer 51**
He, Her, Hero and, finally, Heroine.

**Test Four; Answer 52**
The train for Westlea arrives one minute before the train for Eastlea. Therefore there is a nine-minute wait for one and only a one-minute wait for the other. On average she will end up in Westlea nine times out of ten.

**Test Four; Answer 53**
Oddly enough, the answer is TYPEWRITER.

**Test Four; Answer 54**
A discovered check.

**Test Four; Answer 55**
A = 7, E = 1, N = 6, T = 4. Since 7,641 − 1,467 = 6,174.

**Test Four; Answer 56**
12.8 inches (not 14 – the most obvious answer). Imagine the shoe box folded out, draw a straight line between the two points and apply Pythagoras's theorum.

To visualise why 12.8 inches is the right answer, imagine the box is hollow with the ends missing. Now open it out so it is flat and draw a line directly between the two points. The two short sides of the triangle are 10 and 8 inches respectively. By Pythagoras this gives a length of (approximately) 12.8 for the longer side.

**Test Four; Answer 57**
They are placed in order according to size.

**Test Four; Answer 58**
It is the sum of money arrived at by having one of each coin (including £5 Golden Jubilee coin).

**Test Four; Answer 59**
73 years.

**Test Four; Answer 60**
[90,010 + 85,231] × 4 = 700,964.

**Test Four; Answer 61**
90 minutes. From 12.15 until 1.45 the clock will only strike once. When it strikes just once for the seventh time in a row you know that it must now be 1.45.

**Test Four; Answer 62**
They are on Bank of England notes: £50, £20, £10 and £5 respectively.

**Test Four; Answer 63**
Change the first '+' to a '4', i.e. 545 + 5 = 550. Using the line to make the 'equals' sign into 'not equals' is also valid.

**Test Four; Answer 64**
I am 45 years old. My father is 81, my daughter is 9 and my son is 1.

**Test Four; Answer 65**
9 (numbers across the top of a clock face).

**Test Four; Answer 66**
H = 9, P = 1, R = 0, O = 2, C = 8, U = 3, S = 6, T = 7, E = 5.

**Test Four; Answer 67**
200 miles per hour. The axle is travelling at 100 mph. The rim of the wheel is travelling at 100 mph relative to the axle. Speed relative to the ground is therefore 200 mph.

**Test Four; Answer 68**
Right, rite, write and wright.

**Test Four; Answer 69**
I and eye, or orc and auk are two possible solutions.

**Test Four; Answer 70**
Gaol and Jail.

**Test Four; Answer 71**
101. They are the numbers which are the same when viewed upside down.

**Test Four; Answer 72**
They are the positions of the vowels in the alphabet.

**Test Four; Answer 73**
The second number is the number of letters required to write the first, e.g. ONE (3), TWO (3), THREE (5) etc.

**Test Four; Answer 74**
The sentence contains ten different pronunciations of the letter 'o'.

**Test Four; Answer 75**
1595. Subsequent terms are created by reversing digits of the previous number and adding to the actual number (e.g. 13 + 31 = 44 ... 847 + 748 = 1,595).

**Test Four; Answer 76**
Cleave, Fast (which mean quickly or stationary – as in stuck fast), or Priceless (meaning 'beyond price' or 'no fixed price').

**Test Four; Answer 77**
The first six multiples of 142,857 use the same digits and in the same sequence, .e.g. 285,714, 428,571, 571,428, 714,825, 857,142.

**Test Four; Answer 78**
Break and brake; great and grate; steak and stake.

**Test Four; Answer 79**
The key is the chemical Periodic Table. Element number 35 is Bromine (Br), 33 is Arsenic (As) and 16 is Sulphur (S). Therefore 35 + 33 + 16 = BRASS.

**Test Four; Answer 80**
100.

**Test Four; Answer 81**
When looking at the component lines which combine to create the numbers of a digital clock.

**Test Four; Answer 82**
65:E and 00:h. This is the read out on a digital clock when viewed upside down.

**Test Four; Answer 83**
They are the 100th, 200th, and 300th day of the year respectively.

**Test Four; Answer 84**
If typed on a conventional typewriter/PC keyboard each letter is adjacent horizontally, vertically or diagonally to the preceding letter.

**Test Four; Answer 85**
Best and worst.

**Test Four; Answer 86**
12,345,679 × 9 = 111,111,111; 12,345,679 × 18 = 222,222,222; 12,345,679 × 27 = 333,333,333 etc.

**Test Four; Answer 87**
Raw and war.

**Test Four; Answer 88**
Number 8. Batsmen 1, 3, 4, 5, 6, 7 are bowled out in the first over; 2, 9, 10, 11 in the second.

**Test Four; Answer 89**
E and N. First, Second, Third etc.

**Test Four; Answer 90**
02.02, 10.02, 11.02, 12.02, 02.22, 10.22, 11.22, 12.22.

**Test Four; Answer 91**
Chill – chilli and chilly.

**Test Four; Answer 92**
Ambidextrously.

**Test Four; Answer 93**
Text messaging.

**Test Four; Answer 94**
Digital clocks gave identical displays for time, date and year, e.g. 20:02; 20 02; 2002.

**Test Four; Answer 95**
$1 + 2 + 3 + 4 + 5 + 6 + 7 + (8 \times 9) = 100$.

**Test Four; Answer 96**
Ell, em and en.

**Test Four; Answer 97**
$5,817 \times 6 = 34,902$.

**Test Four; Answer 98**
Time flies? You cannot! Their flight is too erratic.

**Test Four; Answer 99**
19:59:59 to 20:00:00.

**Test Four; Answer 100**
At the Augusta National Golf Club, Georgia, USA. They are the names of the 11th,12th and 13th holes respectively, and known collectively as "Amen Corner".

---

## TEST FIVE SOLUTIONS

**Test Five; Answer 1**
There are more of them (1,996 and 1,997 are numbers, not years).

**Test Five; Answer 2**
They all have five letters.

**Test Five; Answer 3**
Cinq. Count the number of letters in the word and write that number in French for the next word.

**Test Five; Answer 4**
Crude and Overt (Covert and Rude).

**Test Five; Answer 5**
c). Although the total volume of air decreases as altitude increases, the *ratio* of all the consituent gases remains the same, therefore the ratio (as opposed to the amount) of oxygen remains the same.

**Test Five; Answer 6**
The chair of the PM has arms while the ministers' chairs do not.

**Test Five; Answer 7**
The second group, because all letters in the first group change their form when they go from capital to small letters, whereas all letters in the second group remain the same, only smaller.

**Test Five; Answer 8**
The number of dots and/or dashes in the Morse Code alphabet.

**Test Five; Answer 9**
Cash and cache.

**Test Five; Answer 10**
Drawers.

**Test Five; Answer 11**
That that is, is. That that is not, is not. Is that it? It is!

**Test Five; Answer 12**
SPICE, ICE, and IC (one degree Celcius).

**Test Five; Answer 13**
Tormentor, enticement, underground.

**Test Five; Answer 14**
Lima and Mali.

**Test Five; Answer 15**
Billowy (unless readers can find a better one).

**Test Five; Answer 16**
Ideology and alopecia.

**Test Five; Answer 17**
Behind the steering wheel of my car, with a taxi in the rear view mirror.

**Test Five; Answer 18**
N. Capital letters written with three straight lines.

**Test Five; Answer 19**
8. Write out each digit. The last letter of each word is the first letter of the subsequent one.

**Test Five; Answer 20**
It was a sundial.

**Test Five; Answer 21**
There are 120 such numbers (5 × 4 × 3 × 2 × 1) and the mean number in each position is 5. Therefore the total will be 120 × 55,555 = 6,666,600.

**Test Five; Answer 22**
Only one term, which is zero. Note that the sequence of products contains the term (x – x), which is zero.

**Test Five; Answer 23**
Matchstick and Knightsbridge.

**Test Five; Answer 24**
Withhold.

**Test Five; Answer 25**
Reign – Re(s)ign.

**Test Five; Answer 26**
Around; e.g. 'around 20' and 'a round 20'.

**Test Five; Answer 27**
Inverness-shire.

**Test Five; Answer 28**
Prescribe – proscribe; step – stop.

**Test Five; Answer 29**

67 1 43
13 37 61
31 73 7

**Test Five; Answer 30**
60.

**Test Five; Answer 31**
55 miles per hour, to give a new reading of 14,041.

**Test Five; Answer 32**
Reserved, re-served.

**Test Five; Answer 33**
Sanction.

**Test Five; Answer 34**
$3 \times 9 = 27$ (Twenty's even!).

**Test Five; Answer 35**
Guilt – guilty; jealous – jealousy.

**Test Five; Answer 36**
277 (mountains over 3,000 feet).

**Test Five; Answer 37**
Fructidor and Messidor (months in the French revolutionary calendar).

**Test Five; Answer 38**
Waterfowl. They are collective nouns for wigeons, sheldrakes, bitterns, mallard and pochard.

**Test Five; Answer 39**
Fast – feast.

**Test Five; Answer 40**
A year and a half.

**Test Five; Answer 41**
8 goes into 'a' and 9 goes into 'b'. Line 'a' contains numbers that have similar pronunciations to common English words, e.g. won, too, for, ate. Line 'b' does not conform to this.

**Test Five; Answer 42**
Scent – sent, cent.

**Test Five; Answer 43**
Outgoing and retiring.

**Test Five; Answer 44**
6/(1 − 3/4)). Six divided by a quarter.

**Test Five; Answer 45**
Around the rim of a £2 coin (quote from Sir Isaac Newton).

**Test Five; Answer 46**
Poisson – poison.

**Test Five; Answer 47**
He is the woman's father-in-law.

**Test Five; Answer 48**
They are the same.

**Test Five; Answer 49**
Laughter and slaughter.

**Test Five; Answer 50**
Cupboard and clipboard.

**Test Five; Answer 51**
2/2. If you regard them as dates, e.g. 2 February, 4 April etc, then all will fall on the same weekday of any year except 2/2.

**Test Five; Answer 52**
Maine.

**Test Five; Answer 53**
Veracity and duplicity.

**Test Five; Answer 54**
ONE HUG is an anagram of ENOUGH.

**Test Five; Answer 55**
At the eleventh hour.

**Test Five; Answer 56**
123 − 45 − 67 + 89 = 100.

**Test Five; Answer 57**
Sequoia.

**Test Five; Answer 58**
18. Successive square numbers with the digits reversed.

**Test Five; Answer 59**
Large, regal, lager, glare, Elgar.

**Test Five; Answer 60**
$8,169 \times 3 = 24,507$.

**Test Five; Answer 61**
They are all spelt differently in the US (ax, defense, specialty, draft, molt, vise, color).

**Test Five; Answer 62**
Alaska; Hawaii; Alaska and Alaska. (Alaska's Aleutian chain of islands actually crosses the 180 degree meridian and therefore puts Alaska in both the western *and* the eastern hemisphere.)

**Test Five; Answer 63**
$99 + 9/9 = 100$.

**Test Five; Answer 64**
TON.

**Test Five; Answer 65**
SPEAR, the other words being asper, pares, parse, pears, prase, rapes, reaps and spare.

**Test Five; Answer 66**
Items, Mites, Times, Emits, Smite.

**Test Five; Answer 67**
A – Draw; B – Ward; C – Back.

**Test Five; Answer 68**
121 is missing. They each represent 16 expressed in bases from 16 down to 1.

**Test Five; Answer 69**
Those days never existed so nothing happened. At that time the Julian calendar was substituted by the Gregorian calendar and subsequently those days disappeared.

**Test Five; Answer 70**
Keats takes Kate's skate and steak.

**Test Five; Answer 71**
The number of lines making up a TV screen picture.

**Test Five; Answer 72**
Think, thick, trick, track, trait, train, brain.

**Test Five; Answer 73**
Oxygen, saxophone, awkward, syzygy.

**Test Five; Answer 74**
A quarter to midnight (digital clock times: 0123, 1234, 2345).

**Test Five; Answer 75**
An abomination of monks.

**Test Five; Answer 76**
Forty is the only number with its letters in alphabetical order.

**Test Five; Answer 77**
They are all ex Prime Ministers: Marquis of Salisbury, Duke of Newcastle, Lord Liverpool, Lord Derby, Lord Aberdeen.

**Test Five; Answer 78**
22. (The hour hand goes round twice.)

**Test Five; Answer 79**
It's in alphabetical order (with 0 = nought; unless you call 0 zero, in which case it's at the end!).

**Test Five; Answer 80**
Spendthrift.

**Test Five; Answer 81**
8. They are the number of letters in the words of the question.

**Test Five; Answer 82**
Emphasis on the first syllable makes a noun, emphasis on the second makes a verb.

**Test Five; Answer 83**
Lilleshall (Shropshire) and Nunnington (North Yorkshire).

**Test Five; Answer 84**
Agamemnon.

**Test Five; Answer 85**
10 to 10 = 9.50 (time).

**Test Five; Answer 86**
One solution is DRINK, DRANK, FRANK, FLANK, FLASK, FLASH, CLASH, CRASH.

**Test Five; Answer 87**
5,318,804 = hobbies.

**Test Five; Answer 88**
Underground.

**Test Five; Answer 89**
Two Brains Raymond Keene.

**Test Five; Answer 90**
They are all self defining except Verb, e.g. 'Word' is a word. 'Noun' is a noun; 'TLA' is a TLA. 'Not a sentence' is not a sentence. However 'verb' is not a verb.

**Test Five; Answer 91**
6. The numbers refer to the numbers of 'bars' lit for each digit from 1 to 8 on a standard digital display. The number for 9 is 6.

**Test Five; Answer 92**
Their chemical symbols (Au, Fe, Pb, Hg, K, Ag) are NOT abbreviations of their English names.

**Test Five; Answer 93**
'Stewardesses' is normally typed with the left hand (hence sinister i.e. left-handed).

**Test Five; Answer 94**
They are all collective nouns for birds:

a bouquet of pheasants
a charm of finches or hummingbirds
a kettle of hawks

a parliament of owls
a raft of auks, coots or ducks
a wedge of swans or geese

**Test Five; Answer 95**
2 (number of characters in Roman numerals I,II,III, IV,V etc.).

**Test Five; Answer 96**
2,520, 2,520, the sequence being the least common multiples of 1, 1&2, 1&2&3, 1&2&3&4 etc.

**Test Five; Answer 97**
71,077,345 (Shell Oil).

**Test Five; Answer 98**
Software (= FAR + TWO ES).

**Test Five; Answer 99**
They all contain an animal: BeRATe, medalLION, sCATter, pASSing, canAPE.

**Test Five; Answer 100**
Boy's names: Colin, Peter, Lance, Brian, James.

## TEST SIX SOLUTIONS

**Test Six; Answer 1**
238,857 miles, on average (the Southern Sea, or Mare Australe, is on the Moon).

**Test Six; Answer 2**
All the words have a number in the letters, but only weightless has eight going forward.

**Test Six; Answer 3**
They are five of the nine orders of angels.

**Test Six; Answer 4**
Angels, archangels, seraphim, and cherubim.

**Test Six; Answer 5**
TUB – BUTT.

**Test Six; Answer 6**
It is an anachronism. Since they did not know it was BC at the time the coin was minted it is therefore a fake.

**Test Six; Answer 7**
Syzygy.

**Test Six; Answer 8**
Remove the vowels and you get: a DVD is bigger than a MD (minidisc) but smaller than an LP.

**Test Six; Answer 9**
It uses all the Roman numerals once in descending order: MDCLXVI.

**Test Six; Answer 10**
Melon. All the others can be converted into longer words by prefixing them with the letter 'P'

**Test Six; Answer 11**
Kerala (South India). The language is Malayalam.

**Test Six; Answer 12**
Cairo – the only one which does not begin with the same letter as the country in which it is situated.

**Test Six; Answer 13**
Sovereignty.

**Test Six; Answer 14**
Xray. Ra is a God.

**Test Six; Answer 15**
France (cinq, six, sept, huit).

**Test Six; Answer 16**
Prison & jail, prisoner & jailer.

**Test Six; Answer 17**
Eagles – the only one to be spelt normally when used as the name of a pop group (The Eagles, Gorillaz, The Monkees, The Byrds, The Beatles.).

**Test Six; Answer 18**
Portcullis.

**Test Six; Answer 19**
Hip, Hip. (Hooray!)

**Test Six; Answer 20**
The numbers 1–100 are all written without using the latter 'a'.

**Test Six; Answer 21**
*Antony and Cleopatra* and *Othello*.

**Test Six; Answer 22**
Churchill is the only one not to have an airport named after him.

**Test Six; Answer 23**
A president and a prime minister.

**Test Six; Answer 24**
One. Colours on their national flags. Libya's is plain green.

**Test Six; Answer 25**
He spoke from Twenty Two to Two to Two Twenty Two to Twenty Two People (i.e he spoke from 22 minutes before 2 o'clock to 22 minutes past 2 o'clock to 22 people).

**Test Six; Answer 26**
An equal.

**Test Six; Answer 27**
On your Microsoft PC screen.

**Test Six; Answer 28**
20.

**Test Six; Answer 29**
No other word in the English language rhymes with them.

**Test Six; Answer 30**
When they are the names of Royal Navy warships to distinguish them from common words.

**Test Six; Answer 31**
BID, bid.

**Test Six; Answer 32**
One letter occurs once (n), two letters twice (pp, tt) and three thrice (ooo, sss, iii).

**Test Six; Answer 33**
Fünf (German numbers; homophones for vier, fünf, sechs).

**Test Six; Answer 34**
The match.

**Test Six; Answer 35**
It means you're driving on the wrong side of the road. (The carriageway marking should read SLOW.)

**Test Six; Answer 36**
Kai is eaten. The remaining four are drinks.

**Test Six; Answer 37**
palest, palets, pastel, petals, plates, pleats, septal, staple, tepals.

**Test Six; Answer 38**
Paper sizes: A3, A4, A5.

**Test Six; Answer 39**
200. Coins of the realm, in pence, in order of increasing diameter.

**Test Six; Answer 40**
F (fluorine). Letters of the symbols of the chemical elements in the first two rows of the Periodic Table.

**Test Six; Answer 41**
Glttny. Seven deadly sins, but without their vowels.

**Test Six; Answer 42**
They are parts of names of the planets in the solar system: Mercury, Venus etc.

**Test Six; Answer 43**
Their two-letter postal abbreviation give the letters for chemical elements. All except Kentucky (KY).

**Test Six; Answer 44**
Hurricane. All are used to describe wind on the Beaufort Scale.

**Test Six; Answer 45**
A, B, C and D can make BC and AD.

**Test Six; Answer 46**
They all contain letters (in order) which make up a shorter synonym: idle, apt, use.

**Test Six; Answer 47**
MILL – Roman numerals (1000 – M, I – 1, 50 – L).

**Test Six; Answer 48**
Arrhythmy (lack of rhythm).

**Test Six; Answer 49**
A pack of cards: 4 suits, 13 cards in each suit, 52 cards in total. Finally, if you count Ace as one and Jack, Queen and King as 11, 12 and 13, then the sum of all 52 cards is 364.

**Test Six; Answer 50**
They can all be silent at the start of a word, e.g. gnome, knowledge, mnemonic, psychology and wrong.

**Test Six; Answer 51**
They all mean 'two', respectively in Russian, French, German, Italian and Spanish.

**Test Six; Answer 52**
Palindrome. Haydn's Symphony No. 47 in G is nicknamed "the Palindrome". Jonson is credited with coining the term "palindrome", and Robert Schenkman assumed the palindromic stage name of Robert Trebor.

**Test Six; Answer 53**
TH. 1st, 2nd, 3rd, 4th, 5th.

**Test Six; Answer 54**
Pray – prayer.

**Test Six; Answer 55**
The second word can be pronounced in two ways, the first in only one.

**Test Six; Answer 56**
In each word anything sounding like a number in English has been written in Latin. Thus: wonder, cartoon, forgotten, great.

**Test Six; Answer 57**
Prion. This is a protein implicated in BSE. The others are sub-atomic particles.

**Test Six; Answer 58**
The syllables of each word sound like individual letters, e.g. RT, XL, GODC, Q, NE, VNA.

**Test Six; Answer 59**
127. Take 1 cell at the centre of a honeycomb: around it is a ring of six cells, followed by 12, 18, 24 etc.

**Test Six; Answer 60**
Start both together. When the 5-minute runs out, turn it over. When the 7-minute runs out, turn it over. When the 5-minute runs out again, turn the 7-minute over. This will have run for 3 minutes, which can then be 'added' to the 10 already gone.

**Test Six; Answer 61**
53 becomes 35 (3x16+5=53).

**Test Six; Answer 62**
Porter is the only word that does not begin with consecutive letters of the alphabet.

**Test Six; Answer 63**
They are the only letters to require four presses when texting.

**Test Six; Answer 64**
The answers are 'small pica' and 'pica'. They are the old names of type sizes formerly used by books and newspapers, and now replaced by the system of points.

**Test Six; Answer 65**
A shepherd who uses a crook; a theave is a young lamb.

**Test Six; Answer 66**
A metal caster, they are both terms used in the process of tidying up a cast straight from the mould.

**Test Six; Answer 67**
Elsa. Seal, sale, leas, lase, ales.

**Test Six; Answer 68**
110. The first six numbers written in binary notation.

**Test Six; Answer 69**
The common abbreviation for each is two consecutive letters of the alphabet: vw, op, cd, st, no.

**Test Six; Answer 70**
They all are, or sound like, abbreviated names of counties.

**Test Six; Answer 71**
They are all dates: Before Christ, Anno Domini and (for non-Christian faiths) Common Era and Before Common Era.

**Test Six; Answer 72**
9 (numbers across the top of a clock face).

**Test Six; Answer 73**
A rowing VIII. Traditionally oarsmen 2–7 are numbered while X is the bow and Y is the stroke.

**Test Six; Answer 74**
Atom. A to M.

**Test Six; Answer 75**
Fingerprint.

**Test Six; Answer 76**
The suffix '-ist'.

**Test Six; Answer 77**
CIVIL, CIVIC, MIMIC, LIVID, VIVID.

**Test Six; Answer 78**
They are the capitals of the only five countries of the world with single-syllable names (Greece, Spain, Chad, Laos, France).

**Test Six; Answer 79**
They are in alphabetical order (eight, five, four etc.).

**Test Six; Answer 80**
Blond/blonde is the only commonly used adjective in English that is variable. So The Girl should have been Blonde.

**Test Six; Answer 81**
One letter can be removed without changing the meaning, e.g. clean, whine, tail, rude, boil.

**Test Six; Answer 82**
BAR. If you add 'Chester' to the others you get actual English cathedral cities. Barchester is fictional.

**Test Six; Answer 83**
Number of official languages.

**Test Six; Answer 84**
Eton (E to N).

**Test Six; Answer 85**
MUMBO JUMBO.

**Test Six; Answer 86**
They are vitamins A–E.

**Test Six; Answer 87**
Bone fractures.

**Test Six; Answer 88**
Make the three-dimensional figure the tetrahedron (this is a pyramid with three sides).

**Test Six; Answer 89**
Kudos. All the others are currencies.

**Test Six; Answer 90**
Patella (kneecap): bones in the human skeleton, from the toes up.

**Test Six; Answer 91**
Boston.

**Test Six; Answer 92**
They are all minor characters in Shakespeare plays.

**Test Six; Answer 93**
Apt, fay, idle, last, mart, rat, roue, rut, save.

**Test Six; Answer 94**
Und – underground.

**Test Six; Answer 95**
In the plural they are all abbreviations for English counties: Bedfordshire, Buckinghamshire, Staffordshire, Wiltshire.

**Test Six; Answer 96**
They are all provided by mongers: cheesemonger, fishmonger, ironmonger, warmonger.

**Test Six; Answer 97**
Clef. All the others form a word when spelt backwards.

**Test Six; Answer 98**
Quest. All the others have two distinct pronunciations and meanings.

**Test Six; Answer 99**
The ship's name.

**Test Six; Answer 100**
Five-twelfths is an anagram of twelve-fifths.

---

## TEST SEVEN SOLUTIONS

**Test Seven; Answer 1**
Neither – There are 20 6s and 20 9s.

**Test Seven; Answer 2**
October – because of the extra hour when the clocks go back.

**Test Seven; Answer 3**
Flammable. All the others have their meanings reversed when prefixed by 'in'.

**Test Seven; Answer 4**
They all make words when put into lower case.

**Test Seven; Answer 5**
A day is a natural event, all the rest are man-made.

**Test Seven; Answer 6**
Only January and October are identical (same length, same assignment of days of the week) in a non-leap year. Only January and July are identical in a leap year.

**Test Seven; Answer 7**
Redressed or Redresses.

**Test Seven; Answer 8**
They are the letters on a keyboard with a raised area, as used in touch-typing.

**Test Seven; Answer 9**
3 'a's, 3 'b's, 3 'c's etc. can be added to make words (banana, bubble, coccyx, dodder, beetle, fluffy, giggle).

**Test Seven; Answer 10**
abc, bcd, cde etc. can be added to make words (abject, backed, cudgel, deafen, effigy, flight, gothic, hijack).

**Test Seven; Answer 11**
Edward (the others all spell words when reversed).

**Test Seven; Answer 12**
Their first names are the reverse of each other (Leon/Noel; Harpo/Oprah; Linus/Sunil).

**Test Seven; Answer 13**
Weather forecast areas in the North Atlantic.

**Test Seven; Answer 14**
Split second timing.

**Test Seven; Answer 15**
mp stands for mezzo piano which means quite quiet.

**Test Seven; Answer 16**
Gallon. British Imperial measures of capacity in increasing order of volume.

**Test Seven; Answer 17**
During each of them there were three monarchs on the English throne:

1066: Edward the Confessor, Harold II, William I
1483: Edward IV, Edward V, Riuchard III
1936: George V, Edward VIII, George VI.

### Test Seven; Answer 18
They all occur in the names of musical compositions: Feeney, Mozart, Holst, Copland, Holst, Coates, Bax and Handel are the composers.

### Test Seven; Answer 19
Row and bow.

### Test Seven; Answer 20
Jamaica. These are villages and counties.

### Test Seven; Answer 21
Karaoke (empty orchestra) and karate (empty hand).

### Test Seven; Answer 22
Aspirin – aspiring.

### Test Seven; Answer 23
Phonetically: AVRE, CD, DK, RT, SKP, XLNC.

### Test Seven; Answer 24
Lustrum – 5 years; chilead – 100 years; indiction – 15 years (they are all definitions of time periods).

### Test Seven; Answer 25
TC (Top Cat and his Gang).

### Test Seven; Answer 26
Five miles. If he starts towards the North Pole and continues beyond it in a straight line he continues from north to south without changing course.

### Test Seven; Answer 27
They are all plurals which become singular with the addition of an 's'.

### Test Seven; Answer 28
Frigate. All others contain a hidden number (two, eight, ten).

### Test Seven; Answer 29
Immunosuppression.

### Test Seven; Answer 30
Herr Wagner, do you spell your name with a V?

**Test Seven; Answer 31**
6. The number of letters in 11.

**Test Seven; Answer 32**
Flibbertigibbet, Whippersnapper.

**Test Seven; Answer 33**
What. All the others rhyme with the numbers one to ten, in order.

**Test Seven; Answer 34**
Beekeeper.

**Test Seven; Answer 35**
64 and 15,625.

**Test Seven; Answer 36**
Arm, ear, eye, gum, hip, jaw, leg, lip, rib and toe.

**Test Seven; Answer 37**
5, 1, 3 .... (values of the Scrabble tiles A, B, C etc.).

**Test Seven; Answer 38**
They are middle names of the US presidents: Warren G Harding, Harry S Truman and Gerald R. Ford.

**Test Seven; Answer 39**
Fire extinguishers. The colour denotes the contents and the letters denote the class of fire on which they may be used.

**Test Seven; Answer 40**
A navigational chart. The circle denotes your position obtained by a positive fix and the triangle an estimated position.

**Test Seven; Answer 41**
They all sound like French words.

**Test Seven; Answer 42**
When it is Times Two.

**Test Seven; Answer 43**
Woolloomooloo (Bay in Sidney, where Russell Crowe lives).

**Test Seven; Answer 44**
Bricklehampton, Worcestershire.

**Test Seven; Answer 45**
They are all names of horses that won the Derby, in 1794, 1804, 1812, 1816, 1821, 1822, 1842, 1862, 1905, 2001.

**Test Seven; Answer 46**
Ireland and Iceland.

**Test Seven; Answer 47**
J. They are the initial letters of the months, beginning from July.

**Test Seven; Answer 48**
Cromwell; all the others are state capitals in the USA.

**Test Seven; Answer 49**
(B)lair and (E)den.

**Test Seven; Answer 50**
Their capitals all begin with the letter B: Bloemfontein, Berlin, Bandar Seri Begawan, Belfast, Buenos Aires, Baghdad.

**Test Seven; Answer 51**
Straightforward, aioli.

**Test Seven; Answer 52**
Diamond (baseball), square (cricket), circle (athletics – shot, discus etc.).

**Test Seven; Answer 53**
Alfa Romeo.

**Test Seven; Answer 54**
Christ Church (Oxford) and King's (Cambridge). The others are colleges at both universities.

**Test Seven; Answer 55**
Neologisms (as recorded by OUP/OED) each year 1970–1979.

**Test Seven; Answer 56**
Eagle. 2 under par in golf.

**Test Seven; Answer 57**
78. (Ages were: 12, 23, 34, 45, 56, 67, 78.)

**Test Seven; Answer 58**
In your wrist: the scaphoid, lunate, pisiform, hamate and capitate bones.

**Test Seven; Answer 59**
Josef Stalin. The other six can be grouped into three pairs where a first name is an anagram of a surname, Adolf-Faldo, Eric-Rice, Elton-Nolte.

**Test Seven; Answer 60**
Kyrgyzstan.

**Test Seven; Answer 61**
They are irregular verbs forming past tenses by adding 't'.

**Test Seven; Answer 62**
Lambda – Lambada.

**Test Seven; Answer 63**
Cedilla. This is a diacritical mark, which appears below a letter, whereas the others appear above.

**Test Seven; Answer 64**
There are ten possible ways to exchange 10p for lower value coins (e.g. 5p-5p, 5p-2p-2p-1p etc.).

**Test Seven; Answer 65**
'Never odd or even' is a palindrome.

**Test Seven; Answer 66**
The Eden Project designer, Tim Smit, also has a palindromic name.

**Test Seven; Answer 67**
They have two pronunciations, giving different definitions.

**Test Seven; Answer 68**
SAVIOUR and VARIOUS.

**Test Seven; Answer 69**
They can all have any vowel put in the middle to make a word e.g. bag, beg, big, bog, bug.

**Test Seven; Answer 70**
41 minutes: 11.19 less 57 minutes = 10.22  9am plus 82 minutes (41 x 2) = 10.22

**Test Seven; Answer 71**
The letters in each pair can be re-arranged to make a different pair of countries: Israel + Uganda; Iraq + Malta; Liberia + Sudan; Libya + Tonga.

**Test Seven; Answer 72**
They all make new words when doubled: aye-aye, cancan, dodo, gogo, pawpaw, tartar, tom-tom.

**Test Seven; Answer 73**
DN. (The last two James Bond films were *The World Is Not Enough* and *Die Another Day*; the first was *Doctor No*.)

**Test Seven; Answer 74**
Because their names all began with the letter 'H': Rex Harrison, Audrey Hepburn, Stanley Holloway, Wilfrid Hyde-White.

**Test Seven; Answer 75**
Double.

**Test Seven; Answer 76**
Senselessness.

**Test Seven; Answer 77**
Widow (widower).

**Test Seven; Answer 78**
Take one coin from column 1, two from column 2, three from column 3 etc. The number of ounces in excess of 55 will identify the column you want.

**Test Seven; Answer 79**
36. The planets are ranked as to their distance from the sun (Jupiter is 5, Mercury is 1 and Pluto 9).

**Test Seven; Answer 80**
Athlete 3.

**Test Seven; Answer 81**
Ell, em and en.

**Test Seven; Answer 82**
Indium. (The chemical symbols spell out a famous name: Al B Er Te In S Te In)..

**Test Seven; Answer 83**
Karlo was not one of the Marx brothers.

**Test Seven; Answer 84**
Einstein – e = mc squared
Nelson – Aboukir
Herschel – Uranus
Talbot – Castillon
Caesar – Rome.

**Test Seven; Answer 85**
The Coca-Cola Championship: Canaries (Norwich), Eagles (Crystal Palace), Foxes (Leicester), Owls (Sheffield Wednesday) and Wolves (Wolverhampton Wanderers).

**Test Seven; Answer 86**
Abracadabra.

**Test Seven; Answer 87**
Effervescence.

**Test Seven; Answer 88**
Wain. The others are also French words.

**Test Seven; Answer 89**
Wooloomooloo in Sydney, New South Wales, Australia.

**Test Seven; Answer 90**
Only 'for' is pronounced as it is spelled.

**Test Seven; Answer 91**
Times, items, mites, emits, smite.

**Test Seven; Answer 92**
They can all lose one letter without changing their pronunciation: isle, gage, nave, plum, sent, rite.

**Test Seven; Answer 93**
48 years.

**Test Seven; Answer 94**
Tony 4, Sally 12, Mary 4.

**Test Seven; Answer 95**
If typed on a conventional typewriter or PC keyboard each letter is adjacent horizontally, vertically or diagonally) to the preceding letter.

**Test Seven; Answer 96**
Neither of them!

**Test Seven; Answer 97**
In 1892, when they were 44, the year would be 1936 (= 44 squared). Note that those born in 1980 will be 45 in 2025 (= 45 squared).

**Test Seven; Answer 98**
Cacophonous.

**Test Seven; Answer 99**
The answer is rock. All the others are 'beheaded' items of household furniture: table, chair, divan, clock, couch, stool.

**Test Seven; Answer 100**
Kerala (South India). The language is Malayalam.

## TEST EIGHT SOLUTIONS

**Test Eight; Answer 1**
Twice only, at 20:05 and 22:55.

**Test Eight; Answer 2**
The number of sections used to form the small digital figures 0 to 9.

**Test Eight; Answer 3**
Hyphenated. All the others apply to themselves.

**Test Eight; Answer 4**
Moabites (the Moabitesses will constitute roughly half of the Moabites).

**Test Eight; Answer 5**
Anagrams of composers: Haydn, Schubert, Arne, Mahler, Elgar, Gershwin.

**Test Eight; Answer 6**

    1 4 3
    2 0
    5

**Test Eight; Answer 7**
They are all varieties of apple.

**Test Eight; Answer 8**
Around the top face: 1, 8, 2, 7 and around the bottom face respectively under those four: 6, 3, 5, 4.

**Test Eight; Answer 9**
Benjamin. All found on US banknotes.

**Test Eight; Answer 10**
All found in Dante's 'Inferno'.

**Test Eight; Answer 11**
Multiple pheasants, woodcock, snipe and herons.

**Test Eight; Answer 12**
Number of separate times as British prime minister.

**Test Eight; Answer 13**
They are biblical measures.

**Test Eight; Answer 14**
The Faust legend – they either wrote about it, set it to music or illustrated it.

**Test Eight; Answer 15**
Wasps, spiders and sharks.

**Test Eight; Answer 16**
They are widely believed to be the three supreme levels in the world of freemasonry.

**Test Eight; Answer 17**
6 lines. For example: join 1 to 9; join 9 to 12; join 12 to 4 and extend one 'square' higher; draw the diagonal line through 3, 6, 9 and extend to the bottom row; draw a line through the bottom row joining 13 to 16 and then extend one 'square'; finally draw the diagonal through 12, 7 and 2.

**Test Eight; Answer 18**
arctophile – teddy bears; bibliophile – books; tegestologist – beer mats; incunabilist – early books; philatelist – stamps.

**Test Eight; Answer 19**
Aintree (Grand National).

**Test Eight; Answer 20**
A game of tennis

**Test Eight; Answer 21**
blander, blender, blinder, blonder, blunder.

**Test Eight; Answer 22**
If the first letter is removed, the vowel sound is altered.

**Test Eight; Answer 23**
Creature: number of extended sensory organs protruding from its head (tentacles or antennae); number of limbs for locomotion (arms, feet, legs, wings).

**Test Eight; Answer 24**
Papworth.

**Test Eight; Answer 25**
NASA astronauts and their nicknames: Virgil (Gus) Grissom and Edwin (Buzz) Aldrin. [The latter subsequently changed his name officially to Buzz.]

**Test Eight; Answer 26**
Each rides the other's horse over the distance in the shortest time, i.e. race on the other person's animal.

**Test Eight; Answer 27**
Tetrahedron. They are two-dimensional figures, followed by the three-dimensional Platonic solids that may be made from them.

**Test Eight; Answer 28**
Dock's ladder = 8 rungs; boat's ladder = 10 (the boat rises with the tide).

**Test Eight; Answer 29**
auctioned, cautioned, education.

**Test Eight; Answer 30**
GNU, KNEW, NEUter, NEW, NUde, NUIsance, PNEUmonia, venue.

**Test Eight; Answer 31**
Touche. The first three are ballet terms the last one is fencing.

**Test Eight; Answer 32**
Savoy Court in front of the Savoy Hotel adjacent to the Savoy Theatre.

**Test Eight; Answer 33**
A bench of bishops: Canterbury, York, Peterborough and Rochester.

**Test Eight; Answer 34**
Falconry.

**Test Eight; Answer 35**
They are all spelt differently in the US.

**Test Eight; Answer 36**
Laughter and slaughter.

**Test Eight; Answer 37**
XL: extra large, Microsoft Excel icon, 40 in Roman numerals, respectively.

**Test Eight; Answer 38**
The arithmetic is being performed on the number of letters in each word:
two(3) + ten(3) = twenty(6); two(3) × ten(3) = seventeen(9); seventeen(9) – two(3) = eleven(6); seventeen(9) ÷ two(3) = two(3); two(3) + two(3) = eleven(6).

**Test Eight; Answer 39**
A river.

**Test Eight; Answer 40**
A table or a bed.

**Test Eight; Answer 41**
Net, owt, xis, eno. All of these are three-letter numbers, spelt backwards.

**Test Eight; Answer 42**
Au revoir.

**Test Eight; Answer 43**
BA and KLM.

**Test Eight; Answer 44**
Two. One spiral one on each side.

**Test Eight; Answer 45**
They may be rewritten with accents or diacritical marks over vowels: Ångström, blessèd, début, exposé, lamé, naïve, résumé, rôle, Zaïre.

**Test Eight; Answer 46**
Cosmology – Dark Matter. WIMP (Weakly Interacting Massive Particle) and MACHO (MAssive Compact Halo Object) are alternative hypotheses to explain the small proportion of observable mass in the Universe.

**Test Eight; Answer 47**
Types of football: American, Australian Rules, Rugby League and Union.

**Test Eight; Answer 48**
Base (nucleotide) pairs in DNA [A = adenine; T = thymine; C = cytosine; G = guanine].

**Test Eight; Answer 49**
Prefix each with a hyphenated letter: A-frame, D-notice, F-word, G-string, O-ring, S-bend, T-shirt, U-turn, V-sign, X-ray, Y-fronts.

**Test Eight; Answer 50**
The arms of St George's cross are at right angles to one another, unlike those of St Patrick.

**Test Eight; Answer 51**
International dialling codes: Austria is +43, UK is +44, Denmark is +45.

**Test Eight; Answer 52**
Mechanical writing: names given to early forms of typewriters.

**Test Eight; Answer 53**
*Les Misérables*.

**Test Eight; Answer 54**
The largest such number is 7,641, the smallest is 1,467.
7,641 − 1,467 = 6,174. There is no other four digit combination which does this.

**Test Eight; Answer 55**
Pronunciation. Beirut and Bayreuth may be pronounced in the same way.

**Test Eight; Answer 56**
Beetle. The first member of each pair is used adjectivally to specify the creature of the second, different species; i.e. whale shark, zebra fish, stag beetle.

**Test Eight; Answer 57**
The reorganisation of BBC radio, from the Light and Third Programmes, and Home Service, to Radios 1–4.

**Test Eight; Answer 58**
Rabbit (authors and songwriters): Harry (Rabbit) Angstrom novels, the novel *Watership Down* and its rabbit community, and the 1981 hit single 'Rabbit', respectively.

**Test Eight; Answer 59**
Effervescence.

**Test Eight; Answer 60**
Lower (glower), earth (hearth), slander (islander), aunt (jaunt), eyed (keyed), over (lover), allow (mallow), ether (nether), dour (odour), lease (please).

**Test Eight; Answer 61**
X, N, T, E, N (last letters of the cardinal numbers: one, two, three, etc.).

**Test Eight; Answer 62**
A (Lockheed) Blackbird did 2,193mph in 1976.
Donald Campbell's Bluebird did 200mph in 1967.
Mallard set the world steam locomotive record of 126mph in 1938.
A (Reliant) Robin car would probably do about 60mph.

**Test Eight; Answer 63**
Camelopard, the old name for giraffe. The others are types of camel or llama, which are themselves related.

**Test Eight; Answer 64**
hip > phi.

**Test Eight; Answer 65**
Conversion between Fahrenheit and Centigrade temperature scales: e.g. boiling point of water, F = 212, C = 100; freezing point of water, F = 32, C = 0.

**Test Eight; Answer 66**
Monopoly: the former appear on the game board; the latter do not.

**Test Eight; Answer 67**
Rock music styles.

**Test Eight; Answer 68**
Pluton: the proposed name for an astronomical body, intermediate in size between asteroid and planet. The others are subatomic particles.

**Test Eight; Answer 69**
8 years.

**Test Eight; Answer 70**
In physics/cosmology, GUT (Grand Unified Theory) and TOE (Theory Of Everything) seek to combine all of the forces of nature; 42 is the answer to the Ultimate Question of Life, the Universe, and Everything, in the *Hitchhikers' Guide to the Galaxy* series.

**Test Eight; Answer 71**
Elision, which is related to pronunciation. The others are figures of speech.

**Test Eight; Answer 72**
Ash (Ashton-under-Lyne).

**Test Eight; Answer 73**
Tendons and ligaments, respectively. The former, usually bone/muscle or muscle/muscle attachments; the latter, usually bone/bone or internal organs

**Test Eight; Answer 74**
Television, TV.

**Test Eight; Answer 75**
Insured body-parts.

**Test Eight; Answer 76**
Deltoid, rhomboid, trapezius (note that quadriceps means four-headed; similarly, biceps means two-headed).

**Test Eight; Answer 77**
Position in the alphabet of the initial letter of the capital city: Algiers, Athens, Ankara; Brussels, Brasilia; Canberra, Copenhagen; Djakarta, Dakar.

**Test Eight; Answer 78**
The highest possible sum of digits displayed (9:59); the greatest number of elements that make up the display – including the two dots (10:08).

**Test Eight; Answer 79**
If you add or subtract a letter to their surname you get an African Country:
Gabon, Mali, Benin, Cameroon.

**Test Eight; Answer 80**
A Toyota.

**Test Eight; Answer 81**
Whale shark, dog fish, spider monkey, elephant shrew, kangaroo rat, horse fly.

**Test Eight; Answer 82**
1965 and 2043. The difference is 78.

**Test Eight; Answer 83**
th again (1st, 2nd, 3rd 4th etc.).

**Test Eight; Answer 84**
Halfback.

**Test Eight; Answer 85**
The number of parts (1, 2, 3) that make up the punctuation mark: (, .), (: ! ? ;), (...).

**Test Eight; Answer 86**
Sandy, Beds.

**Test Eight; Answer 87**
Synthetic: the others are terms used in mathematics to classify types of numbers.

**Test Eight; Answer 88**
They are uranium neptunium, plutonium, named after the outermost planets, Uranus, Neptune, Pluto (if Pluto can still be considered a planet).

**Test Eight; Answer 89**
Caster (sugar) and castor (sugar or oil).

**Test Eight; Answer 90**
Positions in the alphabet of the first and last letters of the country of which they are capital cities: Argentina, Albania, Austria; Bulgaria; Canada; England; France.

**Test Eight; Answer 91**
Equality (e-quality).

**Test Eight; Answer 92**
This represents the ranking for most common use of words in the English language (e.g. the = 1).

**Test Eight; Answer 93**
Hector Berlioz.

**Test Eight; Answer 94**
Normandy (No R, M, and Y).

**Test Eight; Answer 95**
Chord and cord, e.g. chord of a circle, musical chord, spinal cord/chord.

**Test Eight; Answer 96**
Number Eight. Batsmen 1, 3, 4, 5, 6, 7 fall at one end, followed by 2, 9, 10, and 11 at the other.

**Test Eight; Answer 97**
Terminator.

**Test Eight; Answer 98**
They are types of chemical reaction.

**Test Eight; Answer 99**
Brain (meninges, plural; meningitis, inflammation caused by bacteria or virus).

**Test Eight; Answer 100**
Carat, ^. Numeric keys and their shifted counterparts (symbols, marks or signs) on a standard UK English typewriter/computer keyboard.

**Test Nine; Answer 1**
Calculus. The former two developed differential calculus independently (Newton calling it 'fluxions'); the latter, Prof Calculus in Tintin's adventures.

**Test Nine; Answer 2**
7–8 against her.

**Test Nine; Answer 3**
They all have (at least) three anagrams, each starting with an individual letter: item, emit, time, rats, arts, tars, post, opts, tops.

**Test Nine; Answer 4**
Only Prime Even Number.

**Test Nine; Answer 5**
Forty.

**Test Nine; Answer 6**
Ten. (wayne roONEy, clint easTWOod, david atTENborough).

**Test Nine; Answer 7**
They can all be preceded by a letter: E-number, T-shirt, D-day, X-ray, S-bend, U-turn.

**Test Nine; Answer 8**
One (one).

**Test Nine; Answer 9**
Clip. All the others make a word when reversed.

**Test Nine; Answer 10**
The only months which can be written with a lower case initial letter as they are also words.

**Test Nine; Answer 11**
Each pair of countries have flags with the same colour stripes, the first one's going horizontally and the second's going vertically. ie:
Bolivia (horiz) red–yellow–green: turn anti-clockwise 90 to get Guinea's flag.
Austria (horiz) red–white-red: turn either way to get Peru's flag.
Hungary (horiz) red–white–green: turn clockwise 90 to get Italy's flag.

**Test Nine; Answer 12**
Presbyterians (anagram of her name).

**Test Nine; Answer 13**
9 (numbers across the top of a clock face).

**Test Nine; Answer 14**
Beijing.

**Test Nine; Answer 15**
With a capital letter to start and an 's' at the end they become the major league baseball teams of Kansas City, Cincinnati, St Louis, San Francisco and Atlanta respectively.

**Test Nine; Answer 16**
BC + AD = ABCD.

**Test Nine; Answer 17**
Cricket. (A cricket bat is used to avoid a duck.)

**Test Nine; Answer 18**
French Polish.

**Test Nine; Answer 19**
Jane 12, James 3 (in 6 years time Jane = 18 and James = 9).

**Test Nine; Answer 20**
They can all take all five vowels. bag, beg, big, bog, bug etc.

**Test Nine; Answer 21**
Count Basie.

**Test Nine; Answer 22**
Chopin Liszt.

**Test Nine; Answer 23**
'Lager, Elgar?' (Large, regal glare.)

**Test Nine; Answer 24**
UK coins: 1p, 2p, 5p, 10p, 20p, 50p, £1.

**Test Nine; Answer 25**
No. A domino will always cover a white square and a dark square but two dark squares have been removed from the board.

**Test Nine; Answer 26**
In the colosseum in Rome – they are all types of gladiator.

**Test Nine; Answer 27**
Gambling.

**Test Nine; Answer 28**
Spider – an arachnid – the rest are insects.

**Test Nine; Answer 29**
A stakhanovite is a model of hard work. Oblomov, the hero of a novel by Goncharov, refused to get out of bed.

**Test Nine; Answer 30**
All are Napoleonic victories apart from Blenheim which was an English victory against the French by the Duke of Marlborough.

**Test Nine; Answer 31**
Incitatus was the horse made a senator by the emperor Caligula – the rest are early popes.

**Test Nine; Answer 32**
Triathlon, tetrathlon, pentathlon, heptathlon and decathlon.

**Test Nine; Answer 33**
Three ways, six ways and two ways respectively.

**Test Nine; Answer 34**
They are the only two months in which each day of the month falls on the same day of the week.

**Test Nine; Answer 35**
They are home to sports teams nicknamed 'Saints' (football, rugby union, rugby league, American football, Australian rules football).

**Test Nine; Answer 36**
Pismire means ant – the others are ant-eaters.

**Test Nine; Answer 37**
A heretic – they are all heresies condemned by the early church.

**Test Nine; Answer 38**
All are in play titles by Christopher Marlowe.

**Test Nine; Answer 39**
It has 12 faces all of which are equal pentagons.

**Test Nine; Answer 40**
b, a, d, c.

**Test Nine; Answer 41**
The first is a wife with many husbands. The second denotes marriage between brother and sister, while the last regards members of a community as being intermarried.

**Test Nine; Answer 42**
They are names for the full moon in February, July, October and November.

**Test Nine; Answer 43**
The first set of diseases are for the active – athlete's foot, heel and groin. The second set are ailments of the sedentary – computer game players' palm and computer gamers' palsy.

**Test Nine; Answer 44**
Apace becomes Apache.

**Test Nine; Answer 45**
East (cf. West Virginia, North and South Carolinas and Dakotas).

**Test Nine; Answer 46**
The authors' names are composed of three parts, respectively: Erle Stanley Gardner, Barbara Taylor Bradford, James Fenimore Cooper.

**Test Nine; Answer 47**
Backslash, \. The others are alternative names for the forward slash, /.

**Test Nine; Answer 48**
Bono. Respectively: their surname; his stage name; Edward de Bono.

**Test Nine; Answer 49**
Helianthus is the sunflower – the rest are Roman military commanders.

**Test Nine; Answer 50**
Silver birch, platinum blonde, goldfinch, Emerald Isle, diamond-back rattlesnake.

**Test Nine; Answer 51**
Erse – Irish Gaelic – Ireland; Magyar – Uralic Hungarian – Hungary.

**Test Nine; Answer 52**
They each have two homophones: by, bye; pare, pear; prays, preys; reign, rein; rode, rowed; so, sow; too, two; vane, vein.

**Test Nine; Answer 53**
The former are types of average; the latter relate to statistical distributions around the averages.

**Test Nine; Answer 54**
Pasta and tapas ('a past').

**Test Nine; Answer 55**
Won ton ('not now').

**Test Nine; Answer 56**
Equatorial Guinea – the equator passes through all the others.

**Test Nine; Answer 57**
Aga – mem – non.

**Test Nine; Answer 58**
Last. Custer's last stand, Last of the Mohicans, Fermat's last theorem.

**Test Nine; Answer 59**
Green belt.

**Test Nine; Answer 60**
9 kilos.

**Test Nine; Answer 61**
Gaffe + IR • giraffe (IR = Infra-Red).

**Test Nine; Answer 62**
Sebaceous – the others are geological periods.

**Test Nine; Answer 63**
Officially the birthday of all racehorses is 1st January, therefore their star sign is Capricorn, the Goat.

**Test Nine; Answer 64**
All can be prefixed by 'New'.

**Test Nine; Answer 65**
A blacksmith (or farrier). (A frog is a soft part on the under-side of a horse's hoof.)

**Test Nine; Answer 66**
I (eye) + NOSE (smell) • NOISE (ear).

**Test Nine; Answer 67**
Backlog.

**Test Nine; Answer 68**
artesian • Cartesian.

**Test Nine; Answer 69**
Slide rule, a calculating instrument. The others are measuring devices (for time, direction of magnetic north, vertical, angle, angular distance, length).

**Test Nine; Answer 70**
Coney (rabbit/hare) Island.

**Test Nine; Answer 71**
Imago, in the metamorphosis of e.g. butterfly.

**Test Nine; Answer 72**
Half-cocked.

**Test Nine; Answer 73**
They are required for fielding: Bowler, Extra Cover and (the) Third Man.

**Test Nine; Answer 74**
Sin.

**Test Nine; Answer 75**
Control. Control Experiment – designed to provide baseline data; Control Freak – someone who has to take complete charge; e.g. Control-F is often used to invoke the *Find* function on PCs.

**Test Nine; Answer 76**
'board' can be appended to produce a new word in each case.

**Test Nine; Answer 77**
Limbic, relating to the brain's emotional and instinctive actions. The others have connections with (left/right) handedness.

**Test Nine; Answer 78**
42 swans a-swimming, and 42 geese a-laying.

**Test Nine; Answer 79**
364.

**Test Nine; Answer 80**
Beach. The others come from the phonetic alphabet used by the emergency services.

**Test Nine; Answer 81**
Descartes. The others are units of measure (force, pressure, frequency, temperature, power).

**Test Nine; Answer 82**
SIX – > IX – > X.

**Test Nine; Answer 83**
Respectively the assassination dates of: Caesar, Marat, Lincoln, Franz Ferdinand, Ghandi, Lennon.

**Test Nine; Answer 84**
Siam. Names of places, modern and ancient.

**Test Nine; Answer 85**
Richard Nixon's middle name was Milhous; Bart's grandmother shared the name Jacqueline Bouvier with JFK's wife; Theodore Roosevelt had a son called Kermit.

**Test Nine; Answer 86**
Mobile.

**Test Nine; Answer 87**
Settings for TV animation series, respectively: King of the Hill; The Flintstones; Yogi Bear; American Dad; Top Cat; Family Guy; The Simpsons.

**Test Nine; Answer 88**
Oboe. 'Haut bois' in French.

**Test Nine; Answer 89**
I'm just sittin' on the Dock of the Bay, wasting Thyme...

**Test Nine; Answer 90**
The Beatles (James Paul McCartney, Richard Starkey).

**Test Nine; Answer 91**
Bodice; hence the literary styles: science fiction, chick lit, bodice ripper.

**Test Nine; Answer 92**
Darts: inner and outer bulls; plus, numbers 1–20 are divided into four areas each: treble, double, two singles.

**Test Nine; Answer 93**
Upper Rift Valley.

**Test Nine; Answer 94**
They undergo the calving process.

**Test Nine; Answer 95**
Nova Scotia, SE Canada.

**Test Nine; Answer 96**
All were the subjects of famous paintings, but their names are not used in the titles of those paintings. Jean de Dinteville and Georges de Selve were the ambassadors of Holbein's 1533 work *The Ambassadors*. Susan Tilley was the sitter for Lucien Freud's *Benefits Supervisor Sleeping*, painted in 1995, and Jonathan Buttall was reputedly the subject of Gainsborough's *Blue Boy* (c. 1770).

**Test Nine; Answer 97**
Fir cone (conifer).

**Test Nine; Answer 98**
4 seconds. It strikes at 2 second intervals.

**Test Nine; Answer 99**
Spelt backwards they all become names of boys or girls.

**Test Nine; Answer 100**

Mars, because it does not occur. Its orbit is outside that of the Earth, so it is never between the Sun and us.

---

## TEST TEN SOLUTIONS

**Test Ten; Answer 1**
The former are often abbreviated (rom-com, sci-fi, sit-com); the latter are not abbreviated.

**Test Ten; Answer 2**
Because 'thermospa' and 'a posh term' are both anagrams of 'metaphors'.

**Test Ten; Answer 3**
panic • Hispanic; sand • thousand; Tory • history; thinks • methinks.

**Test Ten; Answer 4**
Rodent = Mouse, Ruminant = RAM (random access memory), Reptile = Monitor (lizard).

**Test Ten; Answer 5**
A pack of cards: spades, hearts, diamonds and clubs.

**Test Ten; Answer 6**
Thunderbirds 1–5: TV series and movies.

**Test Ten; Answer 7**
Anagrams of capital cities, respectively: Tirana (Albania), Rome (Italy), Paris (France), Oslo (Norway).

**Test Ten; Answer 8**
Libreville, Freetown: the former is French for the latter.

**Test Ten; Answer 9**
Bango. The others are former Japanese Provinces.

**Test Ten; Answer 10**
Neath.

**Test Ten; Answer 11**
NRA: National Rivers Authority, and National Rifle Association, respectively.

**Test Ten; Answer 12**
Two gills.

**Test Ten; Answer 13**
They have all been inducted into the Rock & Roll Hall of Fame. Leonard Chess, B.B. King, Queen, Fats Domino, Al Green, Jerry Moss, Buddy Holly, Chuck Berry.

**Test Ten; Answer 14**
Valentine's Day. The first and last days of the month are the same day only in February (in a leap year). 14 February is Valentine's Day.

**Test Ten; Answer 15**
unionized → un-ionized.

**Test Ten; Answer 16**
Increasing number of players, respectively: 2, 4, 5, 6, 7, 8, 9 and 10 (Men) or 12 (Women).

**Test Ten; Answer 17**
Google.

**Test Ten; Answer 18**
Yahoo. In *Gulliver's Travels*, Jonathan Swift created them as a satire on human behaviour.

**Test Ten; Answer 19**
In computing, they are 3GLs (third generation languages), respectively: FORTRAN, BASIC, COBOL.

**Test Ten; Answer 20**
Ouija (*Oui*, French; *Ja*, German), board for communicating with the spirit world.

**Test Ten; Answer 21**
Respectively: the river Styx; in the sticks; Pooh sticks.

**Test Ten; Answer 22**
*Romeo and Juliet, Antony and Cleopatra, Troilus and Cressida* and *Titus Andronicus*.

**Test Ten; Answer 23**
April, May and June are girls' names.

**Test Ten; Answer 24**
A trombone, which in French can also mean a paper clip and in Italian can also mean a braggart (or a windbag), a daffodil or a sawn-off shotgun.

**Test Ten; Answer 25**
They are all characters in Shakespeare (in *Measure for Measure, Love's Labour's Lost,    A Midsummer Night's Dream, Comedy of Errors* and *A Midsummer Night's Dream* respectively).

**Test Ten; Answer 26**
Queen. Dannay and Lee were co-authors writing under the pseudonym of Ellery Queen. Lead singer of Queen, Freddie Mercury was born Farrokh Bulsara. Beatrix Armgard is Queen Beatrix of the Netherlands.

**Test Ten; Answer 27**
Butter. 'Milk' may follow it, but precede the others.

**Test Ten; Answer 28**
Précis (pronounced pray-see).

**Test Ten; Answer 29**
Penguin, found naturally in the Antarctic. The others are within the Arctic Circle.

**Test Ten; Answer 30**
Isle of Lewis, and Lewes.

**Test Ten; Answer 31**
Their stage names differ from their original names, respectively: Elton John, Cliff Richard, Michael Caine, Barry Manilow, Billie Holiday, Boy George.

**Test Ten; Answer 32**
to – unto.

**Test Ten; Answer 33**
prison, jail – prisoner, jailer.

**Test Ten; Answer 34**
Because they are two of a set of triplets.

**Test Ten; Answer 35**
Sibling. All the others refer to a specific sex.

**Test Ten; Answer 36**
France (tea or coffee served *au lait*) and Spain (*Olé!*).

**Test Ten; Answer 37**
heroin • heroine.

**Test Ten; Answer 38**
The number of component parts of the corresponding Roman numeral:
I, II, III, IV, V, VI, VII, VIII, XI, X.

**Test Ten; Answer 39**
When reversed, each forms a new word; respectively: are, lived, flog, trap, tops, rats, emit, mart.

**Test Ten; Answer 40**
The letter N: to produce – range, snack, bends, arena, gnash, borne.

**Test Ten; Answer 41**
Take as read.

**Test Ten; Answer 42**
Kite. Respectively: a diamond-shape, elongated asymmetrically; the kite mark; and, e.g. the red kite.

**Test Ten; Answer 43**
Name repetition: Boutros Boutros-Ghali and Ford Madox Ford.

**Test Ten; Answer 44**
Titles of their books contain numbers, respectively: *Fahrenheit 451*; *2001 – A Space Odyssey*; *Catch 22*; *One Hundred and One Dalmatians*; *The Secret Diaries of Adrian Mole, Aged 13¾*.

**Test Ten; Answer 45**
Snake. Snake eyes – two ones; snake oil – fake remedy; snake in the grass – false friend.

**Test Ten; Answer 46**
Bled. The others are all the real surnames of famous people. Frederick Austerlitz – Fred Astaire; Allen Konigsberg – Woody Allen; Doris Kappelhoff – Doris Day.

**Test Ten; Answer 47**
They are all misattributed. The 'Haydn' is by Leopold Mozart; the 'Bach' is by Stoezel; the 'Mozart' and 'Handel' are forgeries by Henri Casadesus; the 'Pergolesi' concertos are by Wassanaer; and the 'Pugnani' is by Kreisler.

**Test Ten; Answer 48**
Charles Buchinski – real name of Charles Bronson. Illya Kuryakin – played by David McCallum in *The Man From UNCLE*. Both these actors were married to Jill Ireland.

**Test Ten; Answer 49**
The skull.

**Test Ten; Answer 50**
HAL → IBM; increment the alphabetic position of each letter by one.

**Test Ten; Answer 51**
Rasta (from Rastafarianism, founded in Jamaica, revering Emperor Haile Selassie of Ethiopia) and raster (pattern of scanning lines).

**Test Ten; Answer 52**
1 September is the start of the partridge shooting season; 30 September is the end of the trout fishing season.

**Test Ten; Answer 53**
They are in respective order: the multiples to convert inches to millimetres, inches to centimetres, feet to metres, yards to metres and miles to kilometres.

**Test Ten; Answer 54**
Only ones to have more than one syllable (2 and 3 respectively).

**Test Ten; Answer 55**
They all contain birds: rEGRETfully pROBINg intRAVENous knowledge.

**Test Ten; Answer 56**
Most number of syllables (5).

**Test Ten; Answer 57**
They are both represented in Roman numerals by just three letters: MMX and MML.

**Test Ten; Answer 58**
1 Joseph Stalin; 2 Vladimir Lenin; 3 Maxim Gorky; 4 Leon Trotsky.

**Test Ten; Answer 59**
Tasted (past participles of the five senses: saw, smelt, he(a)rd, felt).

**Test Ten; Answer 60**
Bobbing (Bob + Bing).

**Test Ten; Answer 61**
All pseudonyms, respectively for Poquelin, Aruet, Dickens and Clemens.

**Test Ten; Answer 62**
Shrewdness of apes; cowardice of curs; skulk of foxes; consortium of crabs; crash of rhinos.

**Test Ten; Answer 63**
Wedding anniversaries gifts. The correct match is Coral 35, Ivory 14, China 20, Tin 10, Paper 1.

**Test Ten; Answer 64**
Manhattan. Respectively: the Project; the cocktail; the movie.

**Test Ten; Answer 65**
All ships which circumnavigated the world. *The Vittoria* was the sole surviving vessel from Magellan's expedition. Sir Francis Drake set sail in *The Pelican* which he renamed *The Golden Hind* while at sea.

**Test Ten; Answer 66**
(Royal Academy of Drama and Art) RADA + R • RADAR (Radio Detection And Ranging).

**Test Ten; Answer 67**
Harvest, the Full Moon nearest the Autumnal Equinox, i.e. late September and early October. The other phases occur throughout the year.

**Test Ten; Answer 68**
Snakes, geese, bees, mice.

**Test Ten; Answer 69**
They may be converted to centigrade by reversing their digits.

**Test Ten; Answer 70**
They are plurals, which are often regarded as singular (extra pluralisation appends the letter S). Original singulars: agendum, candelabrum, insigne, opus, panino.

**Test Ten; Answer 71**
Blake.

**Test Ten; Answer 72**
Vaticide – the others have to be relatives who have been killed. Vaticide is the killing of a prophet, who can of course be unrelated.

**Test Ten; Answer 73**
A nebuchadnezzar – a jeroboam is a 4 size bottle of champagne – a nebuchadnezzar is equivalent to 20 bottles.

**Test Ten; Answer 74**
They are forms of divination.

**Test Ten; Answer 75**
They are the characters of the four kings in the suits in French traditional card packs.

**Test Ten; Answer 76**
spumante refers to sparkling wine-the others are musical terms.

**Test Ten; Answer 77**
Renaissance artists and their works: Leonardo – *Mona Lisa*; Michaelangelo – *The Last Judgement*; Raphael – *The School of Athens*; Botticelli – *The Birth of Venus*.

**Test Ten; Answer 78**
calcium carbonate – chalk; nitrous oxide – laughing gas; sodium chloride – salt; hydrated ferric oxide – rust.

**Test Ten; Answer 79**
They are all anagrams of forms of winter weather: snow, rain, sleet, thaw, frost, rime.

**Test Ten; Answer 80**
Teller (Edward Teller; counts money in and out; a relater of anecdotes).

**Test Ten; Answer 81**
The bible. There are 39 books in the old testament, 150 psalms, 27 books in the new testament and 66 books in the bible in total.

**Test Ten; Answer 82**
Arm, mouth and cheek.

**Test Ten; Answer 83**
Digital versatile disk; random access memory; read only memory.

**Test Ten; Answer 84**
Names of horses belonging respectively to Napoleon, Wellington and Richard III.

**Test Ten; Answer 85**
Vauxhall. All the other names are also common nouns.

**Test Ten; Answer 86**
Eel, hare, rook, kangaroo.

**Test Ten; Answer 87**
Every year contains a repeated digit.

**Test Ten; Answer 88**
The 104 years 1099–1202.

**Test Ten; Answer 89**
They tend to contradict each other:

If you wish for peace prepare for war.
Go in peace.

To understand everything is to forgive everything.
It is not permitted to know everything.

**Test Ten; Answer 90**
centiare, decare, acre, hectare (in square metres: 1, 1,000, 4,046, 10,000).

**Test Ten; Answer 91**
Bee, crow, hare, parrot.

**Test Ten; Answer 92**
The correct order is Mercury, Venus, Mars, Saturn, Neptune.

**Test Ten; Answer 93**
The astronaut Alan Shepard. The golf balls he hit on the moon landed over 200,000 miles from the nearest green back on Earth.

**Test Ten; Answer 94**
In wedding anniversaries. Wood is the 5th, tin the 10th and china the 20th.

**Test Ten; Answer 95**
Tiger, respectively: Eye of the Tiger music in *Rocky IV*; The Tyger 'Tyger, Tyger burning bright'; Tigger, in Winnie the Pooh stories.

**Test Ten; Answer 96**
Bentine (Michael); dentine; pentene, $C_5H_{10}$.

**Test Ten; Answer 97**
36, 36
x1, x2, x3 repeated.

**Test Ten; Answer 98**
16.

**Test Ten; Answer 99**
They are in succession the dates the Black Death reached Europe, the fire of London, the London Plague and the black hole of Calcutta.

**Test Ten; Answer 100**
It is the Olympic motto: faster, higher, stronger.